Growing with Confidence through Compassion with a Spine

A Stronger Way to Heal Without Losing Yourself

Cassandra Wygle, LPC, NCC

Growing with Confidence through Compassion with a Spine

A Stronger Way to Heal Without Losing Yourself

Author: Cassandra Wygle, LPC, NCC
First edition

ISBN: 979-8-9976228-0-0
Printed in the United States of America

For the ones who are learning they do not have to shrink to be safe.

For every part of me that needed to learn it first.

Author's Note

I did not write this book because confidence is a trend. I wrote it because I kept seeing the same pattern in different rooms: people had more language for what hurt, but not always more capacity to live beyond it.

Apparently, my brain does not let a pattern walk by without pulling out a clipboard.

Apparently, this is both a clinical skill and a personality trait. We are all coping in our own ways.

In therapy rooms.

In supervision spaces.

In classrooms.

In workplaces.

In relationships.

In the quiet conversations people have with themselves when they are trying to become sturdier than their fear. The language matters. It can reduce shame, organize pain, and make an experience feel less isolating. Language is a beginning, not a capacity. Naming a pattern is not the same as changing it. Understanding a wound is not the same as healing it. Feeling seen is not the same as becoming able.

Somewhere along the way, comfort began masquerading as healing, avoidance learned the language of self-care, and confidence became something people waited to feel instead of something they practiced. Growing with Confidence began from the belief that confidence is quieter than performance. It is built in hard conversations, imperfect attempts, daily follow-through, emotional discomfort, and the moments when avoidance would be easier. The Professional Integrity Project began from a related conviction: the work must be protected. Mental health care requires precision, standards, accountability, and enough backbone to tell the truth without losing the person in front of us.

For a long time, those looked like two separate bodies of work. They are two expressions of the same standard.

Confidence without structure becomes performance.

Structure without compassion becomes severity.

Healing without accountability becomes avoidance.

Accountability without care becomes harm.

What we need is not less compassion. We need stronger compassion. Compassion with a spine. The kind that does not shame people for struggling or treat struggle as proof of incapability. The kind that can validate pain and still ask what growth requires. This book was written from inside that tension: as a therapist, clinical supervisor, educator, and human still practicing what I teach. I know what it is to want confidence before the step, clarity before the risk, and reassurance before the responsibility. I also know that softness without structure was never enough for the kind of life I wanted to build.

I am not writing from some spotless expert chair where every pattern has been mastered and filed alphabetically. I am writing from the repeated, sometimes inconvenient practice of becoming sturdier without becoming less tender.

Compassion with a Spine is not branding first. It is a standard: care should stay humane without becoming so afraid of discomfort that it stops helping people grow.

Softness belongs here. Shrinking does not have to.

We must protect the work.

We must protect the field.

We must protect the people we serve.

We must also protect the person we are becoming from a culture that keeps teaching us to avoid the very discomfort that would help us grow.

If you are here, I trust you are ready for that kind of conversation. Let's begin.

Reader's Note

This book was written for more than one kind of reader because this pattern is showing up in more than one kind of place. For clinicians, this book offers a framework for protecting the integrity of the work while strengthening clinical decision-making, accountability, and capacity-building. For students and developing professionals, it offers language for the tension you may already feel: the desire to be compassionate without becoming passive, supportive without becoming avoidant, and to stay clinically attuned without losing your standards. For all individuals, it offers a way to understand your own patterns without turning every struggle into an identity or every discomfort into a stop sign.

You do not need formal clinical training to benefit from this book. You do, however, need a willingness to be honest. If you are reading as a clinician, notice the clinical drift, scope issues, reinforcement patterns, treatment implications, and places where compassion may need more structure. If you are reading as a student or developing professional, notice the framework for professional identity, clinical judgment, supervision, and the discomfort of learning without losing your standards. If you are reading for your own growth, notice where the language applies to your daily patterns, relationships, confidence, faith, wellness, and avoidance.

Which is rude of growth, honestly. Honesty has a way of walking in before we feel ready and pointing directly at the thing we were hoping could stay decorative.

Not brutally honest. Not internet-honest. Honest enough that your avoidance cannot hide under a throw blanket and call itself healing.

This is not a workbook or a treatment manual. It is a framework for growth, informed by clinical practice and built to be used. Its central premise is simple:

What you practice shapes what you become capable of. If you practice avoidance, your world narrows. If you practice engagement, your capacity expands. If you wait to feel confident before you act, you may wait for a very long time.

Confidence grows through evidence.

Evidence grows through repetition.

Repetition requires discomfort.

This book will not always feel soothing. It is not supposed to flatter avoidance or decorate fear. It is supposed to help you notice when protection has become limitation, when validation has stopped short of growth, and when compassion needs more structure to actually help. Read it straight through or return to the chapters that become relevant. The Practice Points are starting places, not substitutes for therapy, supervision, medical care, or professional consultation when those are needed.

The Practice Points are not meant to become another way to overthink growth. They are meant to help you notice one pattern, try one action, and measure whether your life becomes slightly more workable. Use them simply. Return to them honestly. Let them move you from insight into practice.

Notice what applies.

Practice what challenges you.

Return to what requires repetition.

Growth in this framework is not measured by insight alone. It is measured by what you do with it.

Contents

PART I

What We Have Been Taught to Avoid

Mental health awareness matters. Maturity within that awareness matters, too. Confidence rarely disappears all at once. It shrinks by repetition.

Awareness without maturity is just a very articulate way to stay stuck.

One avoided conversation.

One postponed decision.

One softened boundary.

One opportunity declined because it felt too activating. One moment where discomfort was treated as evidence that something was wrong instead of evidence that something mattered.

At first, avoidance feels protective.

It lowers the intensity.

It creates relief.

It gives the nervous system a brief exhale. It makes the hard thing go away for a little while. That relief can be convincing. The problem is that relief and recovery are not the same thing.

Relief asks, "How do I feel right now?"

Recovery asks, "What am I becoming able to do?"

We are living in a culture that has become very skilled at naming discomfort and less practiced at building capacity for it. Mental health has never been more visible. That visibility has helped people name pain, question old systems, and seek support. It has also made complex clinical language easy to flatten, market, and repeat without enough precision.

Visibility without precision creates confusion. Accessibility without accountability creates risk. Language without practice can leave people with more insight but less capacity. The pattern shows up in clinical rooms, classrooms, workplaces, relationships, and private life.

Discomfort is labeled harm.

Accountability is reframed as cruelty.

Symptoms are treated as identity.

Avoidance is renamed self-care.

Feeling validated becomes the endpoint instead of the beginning. The result is not empowerment. It is shrinking with better vocabulary. People arrive with language, but not always with tolerance. They can name the trigger but cannot stay in the conversation. They can identify the wound but cannot practice the boundary. They can explain the anxiety but still organize their life around avoiding it. They can describe the pattern but still repeat it. This is not because people are weak. It is because what we practice gets stronger.

If we practice avoidance, avoidance strengthens. If we practice retreat, retreat becomes familiar. If we practice interpreting discomfort as danger, the world begins to feel increasingly unsafe. If we practice engagement, something else becomes possible.

Capacity grows. Confidence follows. Part I names what has been eroding: how digital influence reshaped expectations, how diagnosis can become identity, how avoidance can disguise itself as healing, and how being treated as fragile can become its own limitation. The critique matters only if it leads somewhere. This book is here to restore a stronger form of compassion: one that can tell the difference between danger and discomfort, and between relief and recovery.

It does not treat people as fragile when they are capable of becoming more. It helps confidence grow through practiced capacity. That is compassion with a spine.

Chapter 1: When Healing Started Sounding Like Avoidance

I did not become concerned because people were talking about mental health. I became concerned when the language began outrunning the work. Better language can reduce shame, organize pain, and help people understand experiences that once felt chaotic. It can also become a hiding place when recognition is mistaken for change.

It can explain avoidance so well that avoidance starts to sound wise. It can validate fear so thoroughly that fear starts making the decisions. It can name pain without ever building capacity. That was the shift I started noticing. Not all at once; slowly, quietly, until one day, it appeared in front of me with uncomfortable clarity. I was in graduate school, deep in trauma coursework. That week we were studying diagnostic criteria, neurological impact, evidence-based treatments, re-traumatization risk, ethical boundaries, and the responsibility that comes with entering trauma work at all. Trauma work was not presented casually. Trauma work was not presented as a vibe, a niche, a content lane, or a certification badge.

It was presented with caution and precision.

It required training.

It required supervision.

It required restraint.

After class, I was sitting in my kitchen, mentally drained, scrolling Instagram. I remember the contrast more than anything. Only hours earlier, trauma had been discussed with the weight it deserves. It was not romanticized. It was not simplified into a caption. It was not treated like a personality niche, a content category, or a quick tool someone could hand to strangers without knowing their history, symptoms, risk factors, support system, or level of functioning. In class, trauma work had weight. Online, it looked effortless. That contrast is what made the moment feel so jarring. I was moving from a space where every word carried clinical responsibility into a space where complex psychological material could be packaged in soft lighting, paired with calming music, and offered as if accessibility alone made it safe.

What unsettled me was not that someone was talking about trauma. It was that trauma work was being made to look simple. A woman spoke calmly into the camera against a soft, aesthetic background. The caption read, "A simple trauma healing skill anyone can use." She demonstrated dissociation as a technique, describing mentally leaving your body as a way to escape traumatic memories and encouraging viewers to use it to forget what happened. My clinical training and my very low tolerance for pretty packaging around dangerous ideas arrived in the room at the same time.

My clinical brain did not gently raise a hand. It kicked the door open asking, "Who approved this?"

The internet loves a shortcut. Clinical responsibility, inconveniently, does not.

Somewhere, a scope-of-practice alarm started screaming in sensible shoes.

I remember stopping there. The content was not merely awkward; it was dangerous. Dissociation is a survival response, not a skill to practice on command, not a treatment protocol, and not a shortcut to healing. Packaging it as an accessible trauma tool for strangers, with no assessment, containment, follow-up, or clinical accountability, crossed a line. I clicked on the creator's profile. She called herself a trauma expert, offered trauma-healing sessions, and sold modules on rewiring the nervous system. Her only listed credential was a thirty-day trauma coaching certification.

No clinical license.

No supervised trauma training.

No regulatory oversight.

Forget what happened.

Thousands of followers were asking her for help. The issue was not that she was speaking about trauma; the issue was scope.

Education is not treatment.

Coaching is not psychotherapy.

Influence is not accountability.

Education can offer language. Treatment requires assessment. Education can increase awareness. Treatment requires formulation. Education can help someone recognize a pattern. Treatment requires understanding the person, context, risks, symptoms, history, functioning, supports, and appropriate intervention.

That is not gatekeeping.

That is responsibility.

General education stays broad; its purpose is information. The person receiving it still has to decide whether it applies, whether it is accurate, and whether professional support is needed. Treatment enters the specifics of a person's life. It requires clinical judgment, scope, training, documentation, ethics, informed consent, risk assessment, consultation, referral when needed, and accountability when the work causes harm. A social media post does not hold those things. A module does not hold those things. A comment section does not hold those things. A follower count definitely does not hold those things.

A large audience is not a treatment plan. It is a room full of people who may need you to know what you are doing.

A blue check is not a treatment plan. I hate that this needs to be said.

Treatment-level language without treatment-level responsibility is not harmless.

It may look accessible.

It may feel validating.

It may even sound compassionate, but when people are vulnerable, hurting, desperate, or frightened by their own symptoms, the difference between education and treatment is not technical. It is protective.

That moment unsettled me, but what followed concerned me more; it was not an isolated example. Over the next year, mental health content multiplied at an astonishing rate. Nervous-system specialists emerged. Neuroscience certificates were obtainable online after a two-hour, self-paced course. Trauma coaches proliferated. Attachment experts offered diagnostic conclusions in sixty seconds. Exposure therapy was described as harmful. Boundaries were framed as abuse. Accountability was recast as invalidation.

None of this happened because people were trying to cause harm. In fact, most of it happened because people were trying to help, sell, simplify, explain, reach, soothe, and make complex clinical material feel accessible. Speed outpaced training, and distortion followed.

At the same time, something else began happening in clinical rooms. Clients were not only arriving with questions, but they were arriving with conclusions.

"I saw online that my anxiety means I was traumatized."

"A coach said I should avoid anything that activates me."

"I read that pushing myself is retraumatizing."

"My symptoms mean people need to accommodate me."

The language was consistent.

The certainty was high.

The distress was real.

Increasingly, functioning was declining.

Clients were more anxious about discomfort; less willing to tolerate exposure. More resistant to accountability; more likely to interpret challenge as harm. Not because they were incapable, but because they had been taught that protection was the highest good. They had been given language for distress without enough structure for growth. They had been taught to monitor activation, but not always how to move through it. They had been told to honor their nervous systems, but not always how to train them. They had been validated but not necessarily strengthened.

This pattern was not limited to therapy rooms or public mental health content. It also entered private decision-making: If it activates me, I should avoid it. If it makes me anxious, it must be wrong. If it feels uncomfortable, I must not be ready. If someone challenges me, they are invalidating me. If a boundary creates guilt, I should soften it. The language changed, but the behavioral result was often the same: avoidance became harder to question.

Validation is often necessary. It can be the first time someone feels believed. It can interrupt shame. It can help a person stop blaming themselves for responses that once helped them survive. It can create enough safety for change to begin; however, validation is not the whole work. If validation becomes the endpoint, the person may feel understood while remaining stuck. If every activation is treated as danger, the nervous system never learns that discomfort can be survived. If every challenge is softened, avoided, or reframed as harm, the person loses practice doing hard things. Clinically, this matters because symptoms do not exist in isolation from functioning. Distress matters, but distress alone does not tell the whole story. In diagnosis, treatment planning, and clinical decision-making, we have to consider severity, duration, impairment, context, risk, and what the person is becoming more or less able to do over time.

Discomfort cannot automatically become the metric for stopping.

Sometimes distress signals:

... danger.

... grief.

... a boundary violation.

Sometimes it signals a trauma response that requires careful treatment and pacing. Sometimes it marks the exact edge where capacity has not been built yet. Good care has to know the difference. A caption cannot make that call. Assessment, context, and clinical responsibility can. Confidence begins to shrink when discomfort itself becomes the stop sign.

Not because someone feels anxious, has symptoms, or needs support.

Confidence shrinks when discomfort repeatedly becomes the reason to stop. It grows when discomfort becomes something a person can meet with support, structure, and repeated practice. Confidence is not built by pretending nothing hurts.

It is not built by shaming yourself into action. It is not built by ignoring trauma, minimizing symptoms, or forcing yourself through life with clenched teeth and a fake smile.

That is not confidence. That is performance. Real confidence grows when you learn, through lived evidence, that you can do difficult things without abandoning yourself.

It grows when you can say:

"This is uncomfortable, and I can stay."

"This is activating, and I can slow down without disappearing."

"This is hard, and I can still take the next step."

That kind of confidence requires compassion.

It also requires a spine.

Without compassion, growth becomes harsh.

Without structure, compassion becomes permission to keep shrinking. The field was not collapsing dramatically when I noticed this pattern; it was simply bending. Culture was bending toward comfort. Language was bending away from precision. Therapy expectations were bending toward relief instead of recovery. People were bending their lives around avoidance while calling it healing. The problem with bending, though, is that the cost was not, and remains not, just theoretical. The cost showed up in missed opportunities, avoided conversations, delayed exposure, weakened boundaries, lowered expectations, and people feeling less capable in the very places they were trying to heal.

That was the moment I understood that something fundamental was shifting.

Not in theory, but in practice. If the problem was being practiced, the correction would have to be practiced, too.

Not through cruelty.

Not through shame.

Not through pretending pain is not real. Through compassion strong enough to build capacity. Through language precise enough to guide action. Through support steady enough to help people stop organizing their lives around what they fear. Through healing that does not just help people feel seen but helps them become more capable. This is the tension this book will keep returning to. People deserve language for what they have lived through. They also deserve support that helps them live beyond it. They deserve validation; they also deserve direction. They deserve compassion; they also deserve structure strong enough to help them grow. The answer is not to take mental health language away from people. The answer is to give that language its spine back. To return healing to something larger than relief. To return confidence to something deeper than performance. To return compassion to something stronger than comfort.

Language should lead somewhere

Language is powerful because it can give people back a sense of reality. It can say, "There is a name for this." It can say, "You are not the only one." It can say, "This pattern makes sense." That matters. Many people need those words before they can stop blaming themselves.

However, the best language does not stop at recognition. It points toward the work. It helps a person understand what support is needed, what pattern is being reinforced, what responsibility belongs to them, what treatment may help, what boundary may need to be held, what skill may need to be practiced, and what life might look like if fear no longer made every decision.

That is the kind of language this book is trying to protect.

Not language that flatters avoidance.

Not language that turns symptoms into identity.

Not language that makes every discomfort sacred and untouchable.

Language with a direction.

Language with care.

Language with a spine.

That is the work of this book.

This is the work the rest of the book builds from.

Chapter 2: When Diagnosis Becomes Identity

A diagnosis can be a map.

It can show you where you have been, why certain roads have been harder, what terrain keeps repeating, and where support may be needed. A good map can be relieving. It can make the chaos feel less random. It can help you stop blaming yourself for getting lost in places that were never clearly marked. However, a map is not meant to become a house.

The relief may be real. The problem is when relief starts unpacking boxes.

You are not supposed to move in, decorate the walls, and decide the border is the end of your life. The map is meant to help you move. It is meant to clarify the terrain, not convince you that the terrain is the whole story. Diagnostic language can do something similar. It can offer relief, context, treatment direction, support, and self-understanding while also carrying the ability to become limiting when the language that was meant to explain the path becomes the place a person stops walking.

There is a difference between having language for what you experience and becoming organized around it. For many people, diagnostic language is the first doorway out of shame. A person who has spent years feeling lazy may finally understand executive dysfunction. Someone who believed they were dramatic may finally recognize anxiety. Someone who thought they were broken may finally see the impact of trauma, depression, grief, or chronic stress. Language can be relieving. It can give shape to something that once felt chaotic. It can help a person say, "There is a reason this has been hard for me."

That kind of recognition can be powerful. Naming matters because unnamed pain often becomes private shame. Before someone has language, they may build their own explanations.

I am lazy.

I am dramatic.

I am too sensitive.

I am broken.

I am impossible to love.

I am not trying hard enough.

I should be over this by now. A diagnosis, or even the beginning of diagnostic understanding, can interrupt those stories. It can help a person realize that what they are experiencing has a pattern, a history, a name, and often a path toward treatment or support. That can be profoundly relieving. Naming can help a client stop moralizing symptoms. It can help a family understand that a pattern is not simply defiance, weakness, selfishness, or lack of effort. It can help a student access support. It can help a clinician choose an appropriate intervention. It can help a person realize they are not the only one who has experienced something similar.

In clinical care, diagnosis can also matter practically.

It can guide treatment planning.

It can clarify risk.

It can support access to services.

This chapter is not an argument against diagnosis. It is an argument for keeping diagnosis in its proper role.

A diagnosis should bring clarity. It should not become a cage. I understand why people cling to language that finally makes them feel less alone. There are few things more relieving than realizing you are not lazy, dramatic, broken, or impossible; you are responding from a pattern that can be understood. I have needed language like that, too. I have also learned that the same language that gives relief can become limiting if it starts deciding what is no longer possible.

I have also had to learn that relief is not the same as freedom. A label can help me understand myself, but it cannot become the place I stop asking what I am still capable of practicing.

It can become risky when recognition turns into certainty without assessment, and certainty turns into identity. In recent years, diagnostic language has become widely accessible. Terms that once lived primarily in clinical settings now circulate through social media feeds, podcasts, online quizzes, self-help books, coaching programs, comment sections, and short-form videos.

Anxiety disorders.

ADHD.

Trauma responses.

Dissociation.

Personality disorders.

Attachment styles.

Nervous-system language.

Burnout.

Dysregulation.

Emotional neglect.

In many ways, this increased access has reduced stigma. People who once felt isolated now have language for their experiences. Families have more words for patterns they did not understand. Students are more willing to ask for help. Clients arrive with a greater awareness that their emotional lives deserve attention. That is not inherently harmful. The problem begins when language moves faster than literacy. A clinical diagnosis is not a feeling.

It is not a single symptom.

It is not a moment of distress.

It is not a sentence on a graphic that feels uncomfortably accurate at midnight. A diagnosis is a clinical formulation based on criteria, duration, impairment, context, differential diagnosis, and professional judgment. Symptoms matter, but symptoms alone are not the whole picture. Frequency matters. Severity matters. Functioning matters. Developmental history matters. Medical factors matter. Substance use matters. Environment matters. Culture matters. Pattern matters.

The midnight algorithm is not a diagnostic instrument, even when it has frightening confidence and background music.

The algorithm can know what keeps your attention. It cannot know what you need for care.

The algorithm can be excellent at recognition and still absolutely unqualified to diagnose your entire personality before breakfast.

Distress alone is not enough.

That precision is not cold.

It is protective.

Clinical diagnosis requires more than recognition. The DSM-5-TR organizes diagnoses around specific criteria, including symptom clusters, duration, impairment, exclusions, and differential considerations (American Psychiatric Association, 2022). That structure exists for a reason. It helps keep ordinary pain from being mislabeled as disorder while helping clinicians identify when symptoms are significant enough to require care.

Precision does not minimize pain; it protects treatment. If the diagnosis is wrong, the treatment direction may be wrong. If threshold is ignored, ordinary distress can become pathologized. If impairment is not assessed, discomfort and disorder start getting blurred together. Diagnostic language should be handled carefully because language this powerful can shape what people believe about themselves. Without threshold, ordinary discomfort can become pathology. Without context, human responses can be mistaken for disorder. Without impairment criteria, identity can begin forming around experiences that may be temporary, situational, developmental, relational, or changeable.

Online environments rarely emphasize threshold; they emphasize recognition. Recognition feels good because it organizes experience quickly. A person watches a video and thinks, "That sounds like me." They read a list of symptoms and feel a rush of relief. They find a community of people using the same language and feel less alone.

Again, that can make a real difference. However, recognition is not the same as diagnosis. Resonance is not the same as assessment. Feeling seen is not the same as being clinically understood. When that line disappears, diagnostic language can start doing something it was never meant to do.

A diagnosis is most useful when it functions like a map. A map does not become the destination.

It helps you understand the terrain. It shows where you are starting. It helps identify obstacles, patterns, risks, and possible routes forward.

It does not walk the path for you. It does not tell you that the landscape can never change. It does not become your name. When diagnosis works as a map, it helps a person and clinician ask better questions.

What is happening?

How long has it been happening?

How much is it impairing life?

What else could explain it?

What support is needed?

What treatment fits?

What skills need to be built?

What does progress look like?

That is the proper use of diagnostic language.

It clarifies the work. The problem begins when the map becomes the identity. Then the person no longer uses the diagnosis to understand the terrain. They begin to live as if the diagnosis is the whole territory. It stops guiding growth and starts defining limitation.

The person no longer says, "I experience anxiety." They say, "I am anxious." Then, sometimes, "This is just who I am." The diagnosis moves from information to identity. Symptoms move from experiences to explanations for everything. Patterns move from things to understand into things to defend. Capacity begins to shrink around the label. This is one of the places confidence quietly erodes.

Not because diagnosis is bad, or because naming symptoms is wrong, or because people should be ashamed of needing help. Confidence erodes when a label becomes the ceiling instead of the map.

There is a difference between saying, "I experience anxiety, and I am learning how to respond differently," and saying, "I am just an anxious person."

There is a difference between saying, "I am in a depressive episode, and my functioning needs support," and saying, "This is who I am now."

There is a difference between saying, "I have diagnosed ADHD, and I need systems, structure, and strategies," and saying, "I cannot be expected to follow through."

There is a difference between saying, "My trauma history shaped my nervous system and my relationships," and saying, "My trauma explains everything I do, so nothing can be expected of me."

There is a difference between saying, "I have executive-function challenges that require support," and saying, "Responsibility itself is unreasonable."

The first version creates a path.

The second version creates a ceiling.

Ceilings are sneaky; they can feel like shelter until you realize you stopped standing all the way up.

One says, "Here is what I need to understand so I can work with it."

The other says, "Here is why growth cannot be expected."

That difference is not small.

It shapes treatment.

It shapes relationships.

It shapes confidence.

It shapes what a person believes is possible.

A diagnosis should clarify direction. It should not become the border of a person's life. A label becomes a ceiling when it stops helping a person understand their experience and starts defining what they believe they can no longer do. It becomes a ceiling when the diagnosis is used to end the conversation instead of guide the work. It becomes a ceiling when support becomes exemption from growth. It becomes a ceiling when every challenge is interpreted as invalidation. It becomes a ceiling when symptoms become identity, and identity becomes something the person has to protect from change. When identity fuses with diagnosis, growth can feel threatening. Improvement may feel destabilizing because the person has built language, community, self-understanding, and even protection around the label.

If anxiety has become central to how someone understands themselves, reducing anxiety may feel less like freedom and more like losing a familiar part of who they are. If trauma has become the primary explanation for every reaction, developing new responses may feel like minimizing what happened. If diagnosed ADHD has become the explanation for every area of follow-through, building systems may feel like minimizing the struggle. If depression has become the identity, moments of energy may feel suspicious. If dysregulation has become the explanation for every conflict, accountability may feel like invalidation. This is not because people are manipulative or unwilling to grow.

It also does not usually happen all at once. A person does not simply wake up one day and decide to turn a diagnosis into an identity.

It often happens gradually.

The label brings relief.

The relief brings language.

The language brings community.

The community brings belonging.

The belonging brings protection.

The protection makes change feel risky.

What began as clarity can slowly become an organizing structure. The person may interpret more and more of life through the label, not because they are trying to stay stuck, but because the label has become familiar, validating, and socially reinforced. That pattern needs care, not mockery. Once a person begins organizing around a label, change can feel like a threat to belonging, safety, and self-understanding. Precision matters here. Mental-health language should not become a more sophisticated way to stay stuck.

Its job is to guide care, reduce shame, clarify patterns, and create a path toward greater functioning. That matters even more in a culture where identity language carries social weight. Online, labels can become communities. Communities can become validation loops. Validation loops can become protective systems around symptoms. A person may receive more affirmation for naming the struggle than for practicing change. They may be praised for identifying a pattern without being challenged to interrupt it. They may be surrounded by people who understand their avoidance, but not by people who help them build capacity. That kind of support can feel compassionate.

Sometimes it is.

Sometimes it is also incomplete.

Compassion should help people feel less alone, but it should also help people become more capable. A person is not more respected when we treat their diagnosis as destiny. They are more respected when we honor what they are facing while still believing growth is possible.

Respect means believing growth is possible

There is a subtle disrespect in assuming a person cannot grow. It may look kind from the outside because it lowers pressure, avoids challenge, and protects the person from discomfort. Underneath, it can carry the message: "This is all you can handle."

That message may be softer than shame, but it is still limiting.

Respect is different. Respect says, "I will not reduce you to the hardest thing you carry." It says, "I will make room for your symptoms, your history, your needs, and your limitations, but I will not make them the full boundary of your life." It says, "I believe support matters, and I believe movement is possible."

This is the tone diagnosis needs. Not denial. Not minimization. Not inspiration pasted over impairment. A steadier respect that can hold complexity.

A diagnosis can be real. A struggle can be real. A limitation can be real. Growth can still be real.

When all those truths stay in the room together, diagnostic language becomes useful again. It stops being a cage and returns to being a map.

That is compassion with a spine.

It does not dismiss the diagnosis.

It does not mock the label.

It does not tell people to simply try harder, pray harder, think positive, buy a planner, drink water, or become magically regulated because someone on the internet decided resilience should be cute.

It also does not treat the diagnosis as the end of the conversation.

It asks better questions.

What does this language help us understand?

What does it not explain?

Where is functioning impaired?

What patterns are being reinforced?

What capacity needs to be built?

What support is actually needed?

What responsibility still belongs to the person? What can change with treatment, structure, repetition, accommodation, skill-building, or time? Those questions keep diagnosis in its proper place.

Not as an identity to defend.

Not as a personality to perform.

Not as a life sentence.

As information.

Important information, sometimes life-changing information, but information still. You are allowed to have language for your pain without building a home inside the label. You are allowed to understand your symptoms without becoming loyal to them. You are allowed to receive a diagnosis and still build capacity. You are allowed to need support and still practice responsibility. You are allowed to be impacted by what you have been through and still become more than your adaptations.

Confidence starts growing again when the label stops being the ceiling.

Not through denial.

Through movement.

Not through shame.

Through skill.

Not through pretending the diagnosis does not matter. Through refusing to let it become the only thing that does. Compassion asks what support, treatment, accommodation, structure, and practice are actually needed. The spine keeps the struggle connected to movement. A diagnosis can explain why something is hard. It should also help clarify what kind of help may make growth possible.

A diagnosis should help you understand the work.

It should not replace the work.

Practice Point

Notice This

Pay attention to the labels you use most often for yourself. Do they help you understand your patterns, or have they started to define what you believe is possible for you?

Try This

Choose one sentence you often use to describe yourself and soften it back into an experience instead of an identity. For example, shift "I am an anxious person" to "I experience anxiety, and I am learning how to respond differently."

Measure This

Track what the new language helps you do. Did it create more honesty, more responsibility, more movement, or more capacity? Confidence grows when language leads to practice.

Chapter 3: Avoidance Disguised as Healing

Avoidance rarely walks in wearing a name tag.

It does not usually announce, "Hello, I am here to make your life smaller while pretending to protect you." That would be helpful, honestly.

Rude, but helpful.

More often, avoidance arrives sounding reasonable. It tells you that now is not the right time, that you need more clarity, that your body is saying no, that peace matters, that you should not force anything, that the conversation can wait, that the risk is not worth it, that relief means you made the right choice.

Sometimes, it is right.

Sometimes pausing is wisdom. Sometimes rest is necessary. Sometimes stepping back is the most honest, healthy, protective thing a person can do. Sometimes fear learns the language of healing so well that it becomes difficult to challenge.

Avoidance becomes dangerous when it gets convincing enough to stop looking like avoidance.

Not all relief is recovery.

That sentence matters because relief can be very convincing.

Relief can walk in with a clipboard and a confident voice, which is exactly why it gets hired for jobs it should not have.

Relief feels like something worked.

You avoided the conversation, and the anxiety dropped. You ignored the email, and the pressure quieted. You canceled the plan, and your body exhaled. You stayed silent instead of setting the boundary, and the tension passed. You did not apply for the position, send the message, ask the question, or risk the answer, and for a moment, things felt easier.

That ease can feel like wisdom, like self-protection, and even like healing. Sometimes what sounds like healing is avoidance wearing softer clothes. Avoidance is not always obvious. It does not always look like running, hiding, quitting, or refusing. Sometimes avoidance looks responsible or regulated. Sometimes it looks like choosing peace and taking the high road. Sometimes it looks like listening to your body, sometimes like protecting your energy. Sometimes those things are real. There are moments when stepping back is wise. Rest is necessary. Boundaries matter. The body needs care. People are allowed to pause, recover, grieve, and move more slowly when life has become too much. The problem is not rest. The problem is when avoidance starts calling itself rest so it does not have to be questioned.

The problem begins when fear learns wellness language well enough to escape scrutiny.

Fear is very good at branding itself when left unsupervised.

Fear will make a spreadsheet if it has to. A dramatic one, obviously.

I know this one because I have dressed avoidance up before and tried to let it pass inspection. I have called it waiting, thinking, praying on it, needing a minute, being wise, or not forcing things. Sometimes those were true. Most of the time they were my fear wearing a blazer and acting like it had a strategic plan. The hard part is learning to tell the difference.

That is the annoying thing about fear: it rarely sounds ridiculous when it is trying to protect you. It sounds careful, mature, spiritual, strategic, and very concerned about timing. Meanwhile, it is quietly moving the furniture in your life until there is barely room to breathe.

Rest vs. Retreat

Rest and retreat can look almost identical from the outside; what matters is what the pause is doing.

Rest restores capacity; retreat protects avoidance. Rest helps the body recover so the person can re-enter life with more steadiness. Retreat helps the person avoid re-entry altogether.

Rest is honest about limits.

Retreat uses limits as a permanent explanation.

Rest says, "I need to pause so I can return."

Retreat says, "I need to pause so I never have to face this."

Two people may cancel plans, take a break, step away from a task, or choose a quiet evening. One may be resting. The other may be retreating. The behavior can look similar; the function is different. A better question than, "Did this lower my distress?" is, "What did this help me do next?" If rest helps you return to your responsibilities, relationships, values, body, work, healing, or faith with more capacity, it is probably rest. If the pause becomes a pattern of never returning, it may be retreat.

People deserve rest. They also deserve to know when rest has quietly become avoidance with better language. In behavioral psychology, avoidance is reinforced when anxiety decreases after withdrawal (Skinner, 1953). The pattern is simple:

Trigger.

Anxiety.

Avoidance.

Relief.

That relief teaches the brain that avoidance worked. At first, this seems helpful. If something makes you anxious and avoiding it makes you feel better, your nervous system remembers. The next time the situation appears, your brain offers the same solution.

Avoid.

Delay.

Escape.

Withdraw.

Do not answer.

Do not go.

Do not risk it.

Do not feel it.

Do not find out.

The anxiety drops again.

The loop strengthens.

Over time, the brain does not learn that the situation was survivable.

It learns that escape was necessary.

That is how avoidance trains fear.

How Avoidance Teaches the Brain

Avoidance is powerful because it works quickly.

That is part of the problem. When a person avoids something that creates anxiety, distress drops in the short term. The body experiences relief. The nervous system registers the escape as successful. The next time the same situation appears, the brain is more likely to recommend the same response.

Avoid again.

Escape again.

Delay again.

Relief again.

In behavioral terms, the relief reinforces the avoidance. The person is not only avoiding the task, conversation, feeling, or situation. They are practicing the belief that escape is necessary. The task becomes more threatening because it is never approached long enough to be re-learned. The feeling becomes more powerful because it is never tolerated long enough to rise and fall. The situation becomes more intimidating because the person never collects evidence that they can survive it. Capacity declines because corrective experience disappears. Avoidance is convincing precisely because it gives immediate relief while quietly increasing future fear.

That is also why relief alone cannot be the measure of whether something helped. Consider someone who avoids opening their email because it spikes their anxiety. The first time they ignore it, the anxiety drops. Relief follows. The next day, unread messages grow. Anxiety spikes higher. Avoidance feels safer. Relief follows again. Weeks pass. Consequences accumulate. The anxiety did not disappear. It was deferred. Each act of avoidance made the next confrontation larger. The brain learned that avoidance worked. It did not learn that the task was survivable. This same pattern shows up in relationships. You avoid the hard conversation because you do not want tension.

Relief follows. The issue remains, and resentment builds. The next conversation becomes harder because now you are not only addressing the original issue, you are addressing the time spent avoiding it. The brain learns that discomfort is a threat to the relationship instead of a normal part of intimacy, repair, and clarity.

It shows up in work. You avoid asking for feedback because it makes you feel exposed.

Relief follows. Skill gaps remain unclear. Confidence becomes more dependent on avoiding evaluation than building competence. The brain learns that feedback is dangerous instead of useful.

It shows up in personal growth. You avoid the gym, the application, the boundary, the appointment, the budget, the grief, the apology, the decision, the silence. Relief follows. The life you are avoiding becomes harder to enter. It can show up around the body. You avoid the gym because you feel exposed.

Relief follows. The gym becomes more intimidating, not less. Your body does not get the evidence that discomfort, awkwardness, sweat, mirrors, other people, or being a beginner can be survived.

It can show up around money management. You avoid the budget, the bank account, the bill, the spreadsheet, the debt, the number. Relief follows. The uncertainty grows. The task becomes heavier because now you are not only facing the money; you are facing the consequences of not looking.

It can show up around medical care. You avoid making the appointment because you are afraid of what you might hear. Relief follows. Fear grows in the silence. Avoidance does not make the body safer. It only delays information that may be needed.

It can show up around creative visibility. You avoid sharing the writing, posting the video, launching the idea, sending the proposal, submitting the application, or letting anyone see the work before it feels untouchable. Relief follows. Confidence stays theoretical because it never gets evidence from being seen and surviving.

Different domains.

Same loop.

Avoidance lowers distress in the moment while making re-entry harder later on.

Avoidance does not eliminate anxiety. It trains it. Language matters here. If a person says, "I am avoiding this because I am scared," at least honesty is in the room. Honesty creates a doorway. If a person says, "I am avoiding this because it is harmful to my nervous system," when the thing is uncomfortable but not unsafe, the avoidance becomes harder to challenge.

It has been moralized.

It has been protected.

It has been given therapeutic language.

Once avoidance is dressed as healing, growth starts to feel like betrayal. One line in this book needs to stay very clear:

Unsafe requires protection.

Uncomfortable requires skill.

When unsafe and uncomfortable get collapsed together, growth collapses with them. Unsafe situations need boundaries, intervention, support, accountability, and sometimes removal. Abuse is not exposure. Exploitation is not growth. Harm is not a character-building exercise. Trauma survivors do not need to be thrown back into overwhelm and told it will make them stronger. That is not compassion with a spine.

That is recklessness.

This is especially important clinically.

Exposure is not simply doing the scariest thing and hoping the body catches up. Ethical exposure-based work requires assessment, pacing, consent, preparation, and attention to the person's functioning, risk, history, and current capacity (Craske et al., 2014). Avoidance may be protective when danger is real. Distance may be necessary when a relationship is abusive. Rest may be necessary when the body is depleted. Stabilization may be necessary before deeper trauma work. Support may be necessary before approaching something that has carried years of fear. Compassion with a Spine does not tell people to override all fear. It teaches people to discern what fear is protecting them from.

Sometimes fear is pointing to danger.

Sometimes fear is pointing to discomfort.

Good care has to know the difference. Not every uncomfortable thing is unsafe. A racing heart before a presentation is not necessarily danger. Tension during a boundary conversation is not necessarily harm. Anxiety before exposure is not necessarily a stop sign. Guilt after saying no does not automatically mean the boundary was wrong. Shame after feedback does not automatically mean the feedback was cruel. Sadness after change does not automatically mean the change was unhealthy.

The difference between discomfort and danger: discomfort is information that requires discernment; danger requires protection.

The body can be accurate, and it can also be trained by history. A familiar body cue may show up in a new situation because the body remembers old threat, old shame, old rejection, old conflict, or old helplessness. The cue is real, but real does not always mean current danger. The work is not to ignore the body; it is to listen without surrendering judgment.

My body has raised alarms over both real danger and mildly inconvenient emails, so I have learned to ask follow-up questions.

It is not always instruction. Confidence grows when a person learns to pause long enough to ask, "Is this unsafe, or is this uncomfortable?"

That pause creates space for capacity.

Without it, discomfort becomes the decision-maker.

This is how people begin to shrink with language that sounds empowering.

They avoid anything that activates them, calling it regulation. They stop engaging difficult conversations, calling it protecting peace. They abandon goals when insecurity rises, calling it alignment. They lower expectations repeatedly, calling it self-compassion. They stop practicing discomfort tolerance, calling it honoring their limits. Again, sometimes those words are accurate. Sometimes regulation is exactly what is needed.

Sometimes protecting peace is wise.

Sometimes alignment means leaving something that no longer fits.

Self-compassion can mean lowering the demand. There are times that honoring limits is the healthiest choice available. The question is not whether those concepts are valid. Many of them are. The question is whether they are being used to build capacity or protect avoidance. That question requires honesty. It also requires humility, because avoidance is rarely random. People avoid for reasons. They avoid because something feels threatening, overwhelming, embarrassing, uncertain, painful, or too close to a wound they do not yet know how to approach.

Avoidance often begins as protection. At some point, protection can become a prison. The same strategy that once helped someone survive may later limit their ability to live. This is why compassion matters. People do not need to be mocked out of avoidance. They do not need to be shamed for coping the best way they knew how. They do not need someone standing over them with a motivational quote and a superiority complex. They need support strong enough to tell the truth.

Avoidance made sense.

Avoidance may now be costing you.

Both can be true.

That is compassion with a spine.

It can honor why a pattern developed without pretending the pattern is still helping. It can validate the fear without handing fear the steering wheel. It can say, “Of course this feels hard,” and still ask, “What is the next honest step?” This is where confidence begins to grow differently.

Not through hype.

Not through affirmation alone.

Not through waiting until anxiety disappears.

Through evidence.

Every time you approach something safe but uncomfortable, you give your nervous system new data. That new data matters because the nervous system does not update through insight alone. It updates through experience. A person can understand avoidance intellectually and still feel terrified behaviorally. The body often needs repeated experiences of approaching what is safe but feared, remaining present long enough to learn, and discovering that discomfort can rise and fall without immediate escape (Barlow, 2002; Craske et al., 2014).

That is why practice matters.

Insight may explain the pattern.

Experience changes the relationship to the pattern.

I can open the email.

I can say the boundary.

I can receive feedback.

I can stay in the conversation.

I can try while uncertain.

I can feel activated and still choose my next action.

The first repetition may feel awful.

The second may still feel awful.

The tenth may feel less impossible.

That is not magic.

That is learning.

Recovery is cumulative.

Capacity is practiced.

Confidence is built through repeated evidence that discomfort can be survived without immediate escape. The goal is not to eliminate avoidance completely. No one does that. Everyone avoids sometimes. Everyone chooses comfort sometimes. Everyone delays, retreats, softens, distracts, scrolls, and says, "I will deal with that later," while knowing full well that later has now become a fictional country where all avoided tasks apparently go to live.

Population: all of us at some point.

The goal is not perfection.

The goal is pattern recognition.

Are you avoiding occasionally, or are you organizing your life around avoidance? Are you resting, or are you retreating? Are you protecting yourself from harm, or protecting yourself from growth? Are you choosing peace, or choosing silence because honesty feels too uncomfortable? Are you honoring your limits, or never testing whether those limits can expand?

Those questions are uncomfortable.

They are also useful.

The life you want will likely require you to do things that activate you.

Growth usually does.

Healing usually does.

Confidence definitely does.

The work is learning when to protect, when to pause, and when to practice staying.

Not all relief is recovery.

Relief is immediate.

Recovery is cumulative.

Relief asks how to feel better right now. Recovery asks what needs to be strengthened over time. You do not need to shame the part of you that wants relief. You do need to stop letting relief become the only measure of whether something is good for you. Sometimes the thing that helps you grow will not feel relieving at first. Sometimes it will feel awkward, exposing, uncertain, and inconvenient. Sometimes your confidence will not arrive before the action. Sometimes confidence is waiting on the other side of the thing you keep avoiding.

Practice Point

Notice This

Where does relief show up quickly after you avoid something? Pay attention to the situations where you feel better immediately, but your life becomes smaller over time.

Try This

Choose one safe but uncomfortable task you have been avoiding. Take the smallest honest step toward it. Open the email. Write the first sentence. Ask the question. Stay in the conversation two minutes longer than you usually would.

Measure This

Track the action, not the feeling. Did you move toward the task instead of away from it? Did you practice engagement? Confidence grows through what you do repeatedly.

Chapter 4: The Cost of Being Treated as Fragile

Being cared for and being treated as fragile are not the same thing.

Care strengthens.

Fragility management shrinks.

At first, the difference can be hard to see because both may look gentle. Both may involve softer language, lowered intensity, slower pacing, support, validation, and protection from overwhelm. The difference is what the support is designed to produce. Care helps a person become more capable. Fragility management helps a person avoid confronting the fear of incapability. One builds capacity. The other protects the fear of not having it. Fragility is often misunderstood, which makes this difference worth naming carefully.

Fragility is not sensitivity.

It is not emotional depth.

It is not having a trauma history.

It is not needing help.

It is not crying easily, feeling intensely, or being affected by the world around you. A person can be sensitive and strong. A person can have trauma and still build capacity. A person can need support and still be responsible. A person can feel deeply without being fragile. I have never believed that feeling deeply makes a person weak. I am tender in ways I no longer feel the need to apologize for. Tenderness still cannot become the reason I stop practicing courage, honesty, responsibility, or growth. The aim was never to feel less; it was to be ruled less by every feeling.

That sentence has been a personal assignment more than once. I do not want to lose my softness. I do want my softness to stop handing fear the keys every time discomfort knocks.

Fragility is not a personality type.

It is not a diagnosis.

It is not a moral failure.

It is not evidence that someone is weak, dramatic, overly emotional, or incapable of growth. Fragility, in this framework, is a reinforced pattern of treating discomfort as proof of incapability. It is what happens when distress repeatedly becomes the reason expectations are lowered, conversations are avoided, accountability is softened, and growth is postponed. Treat fragility like a character flaw and people get shamed. Understand it as a practiced pattern and people can be strengthened. It is marked by low distress tolerance, repeated avoidance, shrinking behavioral range, and identity organized around limitation.

It is what happens when discomfort becomes the boundary of a person's life. Capability is different. Capability is the practiced ability to tolerate discomfort, maintain boundaries, accept accountability, preserve functioning, and act in alignment with values rather than fear. Capability does not mean a person feels nothing. It means they are no longer ruled by every feeling. This is consistent with what resilience and self-efficacy research have long suggested: people build a stronger sense of capability through supported engagement, mastery experiences, adaptation, and repeated evidence that difficulty can be met (Bandura, 1977; Masten, 2001). Capacity is not built by removing every demand.

It is built through experiences that are challenging enough to require growth and supported enough to remain workable.

That is the balance.

Too much demand can overwhelm.

Too little demand can underdevelop.

Capability grows in the space where support and expectation meet. For years, my clinical work has operated from a simple conviction: compassion must build strength, not replace it. That conviction became one of the anchors of Compassion with a Spine. This conviction would later become part of the larger Compassion with a Spine framework, which rests on five pillars:

Capability over fragility.

Boundaries as care.

Accountability as compassion.

Functioning as the metric of progress.

Emotional adulthood as the goal.

Capability comes first because without it, the remaining pillars collapse.

Boundaries require capacity.

Accountability requires capacity.

Functioning requires capacity.

Emotional adulthood requires capacity.

Confidence requires capacity, too.

You cannot build confidence while repeatedly teaching yourself that you cannot tolerate discomfort. You cannot build emotional strength while every difficult feeling becomes a reason to stop. You cannot build trust in yourself if you constantly outsource your sense of safety to everyone else's behavior. You cannot grow if the only support offered is a lower demand. This is one of the quiet costs of being treated as fragile. The person may feel protected, but they may also receive the message that they are not capable of more. No one has to say it directly. The message can be communicated through lowered expectations, avoided conversations, excessive reassurance, softened accountability, and repeated accommodation without skill-building.

It can sound like care.

"Do not push yourself."

"You should not have to feel that."

"If it activates you, it is probably not healthy."

"You do not owe anyone anything."

"Your feelings are valid, so that is enough."

"You should only do what feels aligned."

Some of these statements can be useful in the right context, but all of them become limiting in the wrong one. A person who is truly overwhelmed may need the demand lowered. A person in an unsafe relationship may need support leaving. A person with trauma may need careful pacing. A person with depression may need realistic expectations. A person with anxiety may need compassion around how hard exposure feels. If the only intervention is lowering the demand, the person does not build the ability to meet life. They build a life around not being asked. When someone builds a life around not being asked, confidence has very little room to grow.

Which can feel peaceful, right up until life sends a group project no one volunteered for.

Confidence needs evidence. It needs moments where the person discovers, "I can tolerate this."

"I can try."

"I can stay."

"I can recover."

"I can do hard things with support."

If life is repeatedly structured to prevent those moments, the person may feel protected, but they also lose access to the experiences that build self-trust.

That is not healing.

That is accommodation without development.

That may look gentle on paper. In real life, it can quietly teach a person to trust the cushion more than their own legs.

In therapy, this can happen when clinicians overprotect clients from discomfort. The intention may be compassionate. The outcome may not be. If a client becomes anxious and the clinician immediately backs away from the intervention, the anxiety learns it was right to escalate. If a client becomes tearful and the clinician consistently abandons accountability, emotional intensity can become a way the work stops before responsibility is addressed. If a client avoids exposure and the clinician repeatedly validates the fear without redirecting toward a supported next step, avoidance strengthens. If functioning declines but the client feels increasingly affirmed, the treatment may feel supportive while remaining incomplete.

Support matters. Support without strengthening can maintain suffering. This is one of the professional risks The PIP keeps naming. When clinicians treat clients as fragile, treatment may become supportive but not corrective. The client may feel cared for, but the pattern remains intact. The room may feel emotionally safe, but the client's world keeps shrinking. The sessions may feel validating, but avoidance continues to organize the person's life outside the room.

That is not enough. Clinical care should not humiliate people into growth. It should also not soothe them into stagnation.

This same pattern happens outside therapy. Fragility can be reinforced in families when everyone reorganizes around one person's discomfort until the whole system becomes careful and silent; and resentful. It can be reinforced in therapy when validation is offered without direction, avoidance is understood but not interrupted, and functioning continues to decline while the person feels increasingly affirmed. It can be reinforced in schools when expectations are lowered without skill-building, structure, or a plan for increasing capacity over time. It can be reinforced in workplaces when direct feedback is avoided because emotional reactions are difficult to manage. It can be reinforced in supervision when developing professionals are protected from discomfort instead of supported through it.

It can be reinforced in friendships when agreement is mistaken for loyalty and discomfort is treated as betrayal. It can be reinforced in online communities when identity around symptoms receives more affirmation than movement toward capacity.

Different settings.

Same lesson.

"This is too much for you."

That repeated lesson matters.

The pattern is consistent.

The person is protected from discomfort.

The person receives fewer opportunities to practice discomfort. The person becomes less confident in their ability to tolerate discomfort.

The world feels more overwhelming.

More protection is requested.

Fragility is reinforced.

This is not because people are weak.

It is because systems teach.

Silence teaches, too. So does rescue. So does the sigh that says, "Never mind, I will do it."

Families teach.

Therapy teaches.

Workplaces teach.

Culture teaches.

Social media teaches.

Every repeated response becomes a lesson about what a person is believed capable of handling. When the repeated lesson is, "This is too much for you," the person may eventually believe it. When the repeated lesson is, "This is hard, and you can practice," something else becomes possible.

That is the difference between handling and holding. Handling communicates, "You cannot tolerate this, so I will manage it for you." Holding communicates, "This is difficult, and I will stay steady while you build capacity." Handling lowers the room around the person. Holding steadies the person inside the room.

Handling may feel soothing.

Holding builds strength.

Handling often rushes to remove discomfort.

Holding stays present without rushing to erase it.

Handling says, "Let me take this from you." Holding says, "I will stay with you while you learn how to carry it differently."

Handling may reduce distress quickly.

Holding builds trust over time.

Handling can make the helper feel useful.

Holding helps the person become capable. That difference matters in therapy, parenting, supervision, leadership, relationships, and self-talk. Compassion with a spine is a holding framework. It does not throw people into the deep end and call it growth. It does not deny real limitations. It does not confuse trauma-informed care with sink-or-swim toughness. It also does not make fragility the organizing principle of a person's life.

It asks, “What support helps this person expand?”

Not, “How do we make sure this person never feels uncomfortable?”

That question changes everything.

It changes parenting.

It changes therapy.

It changes supervision.

It changes leadership.

It changes friendship.

It changes how people talk to themselves. When you treat yourself as fragile, your inner voice may sound compassionate, but it will quietly lower the expectation.

“You cannot handle that conversation.”

“You are not ready.”

“You will fall apart.”

“You should avoid it until you feel better.”

“Other people can do that, but not you.”

When you treat yourself as capable, your inner voice still acknowledges difficulty, but it does not surrender authority to fear.

"This is hard, and I can take one step."

"I may need support, but I am not helpless."

"I can pause without quitting."

"I can feel anxious and still act."

"I can learn by doing."

That is the voice confidence grows from.

Not arrogance.

Not denial.

Not self-abandonment.

Steadiness.

The kind of confidence that matters is not the belief that everything will feel easy. It is the belief that you can remain with yourself when things are not. Being treated as fragile can make a person feel cared for in the moment, but it can also steal opportunities for evidence.

Evidence is what confidence needs.

Not vibes. Not a pep talk in cute font. Evidence.

Evidence that you stayed

, that you recovered, that you repaired, that you tried, that you tolerated the feeling without obeying it immediately. Evidence that you can do hard things without becoming hard.

That is the balance.

Soft enough to remain human, strong enough to keep growing.

The correction is not severity.

It is strengthening.

You do not need the world to shrink for you to survive it. You need the capacity to expand within it.

That capacity can be built. It will not be built by treating every discomfort as proof that you cannot.

Practice Point

Notice This

Where are you being treated, or treating yourself, as fragile? Look for places where expectations are repeatedly lowered, conversations are avoided, or discomfort becomes the reason nothing changes.

Try This

Choose one area where you have been asking for protection when you may actually need practice. Identify one supportive step that builds capacity instead of simply reducing discomfort.

Measure This

Ask what the support produced. Did it help you avoid, or did it help you expand? Confidence grows when care strengthens capability.

Chapter 5: Why Confidence Cannot Grow in a Shrinking Life

A life can get smaller without anyone moving the walls.

At first, nothing looks dramatic. You still go to work. You still answer messages. You still keep the lights on, buy groceries, do the dishes sometimes, and appear functional enough that no one would necessarily call it shrinking.

Quietly, certain rooms close.

The room where you say what you mean.
The room where you try before you feel ready.
The room where you let yourself be seen.
The room where you risk disappointing someone.
The room where you ask for more.
The room where you practice being new.

At first, closing a room may feel like peace. It may even be peace for a season. When more and more of life becomes organized around avoiding discomfort, the house starts to feel safe because there is less and less of it left to enter.

Confidence cannot grow in a life where the doors keep closing.

The saddest part is how normal it can start to feel. Eventually the smaller house seems like your personality.

At some point, peace stops being peace and starts looking suspiciously like a very well-decorated hiding place.

A shrinking life does not usually announce itself as shrinking. It often begins with one reasonable decision. You skip the gathering because you feel exposed. You avoid the conversation because you do not want tension. You wait to apply because you do not feel ready. You stay quiet because being misunderstood feels too uncomfortable. You stop going to the gym because you do not want to be seen trying. You delay the appointment because you are afraid of what you might hear. You avoid the budget because the number feels too overwhelming. You stop sharing the idea because criticism might hurt.

One decision may not change much.

Sometimes one decision is wisdom.

Sometimes it is rest.

Sometimes it is pacing.

Sometimes it is protection.

Repeated over time, those decisions begin to shape the size of a life.

The calendar gets smaller.

The conversations get safer.

The goals get quieter.

The risks get postponed.

The relationships get less honest.

The body gets less evidence.

The work gets less challenging.

The person gets less practiced.

Eventually, what began as self-protection can become self-confinement. That is the quiet cost of shrinking.

Not dramatic collapse.

Not obvious failure.

Just a life slowly organized around avoiding the next uncomfortable thing.

Confidence needs room.

Not perfection.

Not constant certainty.

Not a life without anxiety, conflict, failure, grief, pressure, awkwardness, responsibility, or emotional weather that shows up at the least convenient time because apparently the nervous system does not check your calendar first.

Confidence does not need ease.

It needs room to practice.

A shrinking life takes that room away. At first, the shrinking may be subtle. You stop going places that make you feel exposed. You stop speaking honestly because tension feels too uncomfortable. You stop trying things you are not already good at.

You stop letting yourself be new. You stop asking for what you need. You stop making decisions that require uncertainty. You stop tolerating the ordinary discomfort of being a person in progress. Each choice may make sense on its own. Each one may reduce discomfort in the moment. Repeated over time, the pattern becomes a smaller life.

Smaller relationally.

Smaller professionally.

Smaller emotionally.

Smaller spiritually.

Smaller creatively.

Smaller physically.

Smaller than the person was actually capable of living.

Fragility does not always look dramatic.

It often looks reasonable.

It looks like adjusting goals downward to reduce stress. It looks like avoiding conversations to preserve peace. It looks like declining opportunities that feel activating. It looks like structuring life around minimizing discomfort. It looks like staying where you are competent enough to avoid being humbled. It looks like convincing yourself you are aligned when you may actually be afraid. This is why the language matters. A person can make a life smaller and call it peace.

They can call it boundaries.

They can call it healing.

They can call it knowing their limits. They can call it protecting their energy.

Sometimes that is true. Sometimes it is the most honest and healthy choice, but sometimes the language is covering a quieter grief: the person wanted more, but discomfort became too powerful. So they stopped reaching. I know what it is to shrink in ways that look reasonable from the outside. For a long time, I knew how to soften parts of myself so other people would not misread them. I knew how to make my intelligence quieter, my certainty less visible, my ambition easier to explain, my range more manageable. I could tell myself I was being humble, flexible, appropriate, or self-aware. Sometimes I was. Sometimes I was simply trying not to be judged. Full disclosure, I am still working on that. The difference now is that I ask for receipts. I notice the cost sooner.

I know what it feels like to edit yourself down until no one can accuse you of being too much. It can look like humility from the outside. Inside, it can become a quiet kind of disappearance.

Fear hates receipts. It prefers vibes, assumptions, and a very dramatic legal brief.

That cost was subtle, but real. When you keep editing yourself down to the version least likely to be criticized, you do not become more peaceful; you become less practiced at being whole.

This is one of the reasons confidence becomes so misunderstood. People often think confidence is something they need before they act. They wait to feel ready before applying, dating, creating, speaking, leading, changing, setting the boundary, asking the question, or entering the room. They interpret fear as evidence that they are not prepared. They interpret uncertainty as evidence that they are not qualified. They interpret discomfort as evidence that they should wait.

So they wait. While they wait, their life gives them no new evidence that they can handle the thing. Confidence does not grow because it has no material to grow from. Confidence is not built from imagined readiness.

It is built from lived evidence.

You do the hard thing imperfectly.

You survive the discomfort.

You learn something.

You try again.

Your nervous system records the evidence.

Not perfectly.

Not dramatically.

Steadily.

This is why confidence follows capacity.

Capacity follows repetition.

Repetition requires discomfort.

The order matters.

A shrinking life disrupts that order.

When you avoid the repetition, you lose the evidence. When you lose the evidence, confidence becomes a concept instead of a lived experience.

You may affirm yourself.

You may understand yourself.

You may explain yourself beautifully.

You may have language for every pattern. If your behavior keeps moving away from challenge, your body will not believe your words yet.

The body learns through practice.

The body needs lived proof

The body is not being dramatic for asking for receipts; it is simply not impressed by theory.

This is one of the reasons a shrinking life can feel so convincing. The mind may want expansion, but the body has been rehearsing retreat. It knows the relief of not going, not asking, not risking, not being seen, not finding out. It knows the short-term calm of making the world smaller.

So when expansion begins, the body may not celebrate immediately. It may protest. It may tighten. It may tell you that the smaller life was safer, easier, more predictable, and less exposing.

That does not mean expansion is wrong.

It means the body is being asked to learn something new.

A life widens through lived proof: one room entered, one conversation survived, one boundary held, one attempt made, one discomfort carried, one repair completed, one moment of staying after the urge to disappear rises. The proof does not have to be grand to matter. It has to be repeated.

This is why Part I cannot end in despair. Shrinking is practiced. So is expansion. The same nervous system that learned avoidance can learn approach. The same confidence that eroded through repeated retreat can grow again through repeated engagement.

So can confidence.

This is not only personal.

It is relational.

A shrinking life changes how people connect. If you avoid every difficult conversation, your relationships may look peaceful while becoming less honest. If you soften every boundary to avoid disappointment, you may preserve closeness while building resentment. If you treat every disagreement as danger, intimacy becomes limited to what is easy.

Relationships need room for tension.

Not cruelty.

Not chaos.

Not disrespect.

Tension.

The tension of honesty.

The tension of difference.

The tension of repair.

The tension of being known beyond what is convenient. When relationships cannot tolerate tension, they become fragile.

Everyone becomes careful.

Careful not to:

...say too much.

...need too much.

... ask too directly.

...to disappoint.

...be misunderstood.

Careful not to become inconvenient.

That kind of carefulness can look kind from the outside. Inside, it often becomes lonely. Confidence in relationships grows when people practice clarity and survive the discomfort of being real. Shrinking also shows up professionally. A shrinking professional life may look like wisdom at first. You avoid roles that stretch you. You decline opportunities because you do not feel ready. You avoid feedback because it feels personal. You stay quiet in meetings because you might say it imperfectly. You keep choosing what you can already do instead of what would require you to grow.

Nothing looks obviously wrong.

You are functioning.

You may even be praised for being steady, agreeable, flexible, low-maintenance, and easy to work with. Inside, capability may be underdeveloped because challenge keeps being avoided.

Work is supposed to stretch people. That does not mean work should exploit people. It means competence requires contact with difficulty. You cannot become more capable only doing what already feels manageable. You cannot become more confident professionally while avoiding every arena where confidence would have to be built. A shrinking professional life can be especially hard to notice because it often gets rewarded. You may be praised for not needing much.

For not:

...asking questions.

...challenging anything.

...taking up space.

...requiring feedback.

For not making anyone uncomfortable.

That may look like professionalism. Sometimes it is actually fear behaving politely. Real professional confidence does not grow from staying invisible. It grows from tolerating the discomfort of being seen while developing.

It grows from asking the question.

Receiving the feedback.

Trying the role.

Making the decision.

Repairing the mistake.

Taking responsibility.

Letting yourself be new long enough to become competent. The same is true creatively. A shrinking creative life often begins with comparison and ends with silence.

You do not post the writing.

You do not start the project.

You do not launch the thing.

You do not try the class.

You do not share the idea.

You tell yourself it is not the right time. Sometimes it is not. Sometimes the real sentence is, "I am afraid to be seen trying."

That sentence is honest. Honesty gives you somewhere to begin. A creative life needs room to be imperfect. It needs room to be witnessed before it is polished. It needs room for the first draft, the awkward attempt, the idea that does not land, the project that changes shape, the voice that is still becoming. If every creative risk requires certainty first, the work stays trapped inside the person. It may feel protected there. Protected work does not always become living work. Sometimes the thing you are protecting from criticism is also being protected from growth. Shrinking can become physical or body-based, too. You stop moving because your body feels uncomfortable.

You stop trying on clothes because mirrors feel cruel. You stop going places because being seen feels exhausting.

You avoid photos.

You avoid movement.

You avoid intimacy.

You avoid the gym, the walk, the class, the appointment, the routine, the food conversation, the basic act of being present in your own body.

Sometimes the body needs tenderness.

Sometimes the body needs rest.

Sometimes the body needs medical care, nourishment, healing, grieving, rebuilding, or a break from being treated like a project. Sometimes the body also needs evidence that it can be lived in without constant avoidance. Body confidence is not built by waiting until the body feels acceptable. It is built through moments of living while still learning how to feel at home. Shrinking can also become spiritual or emotional.

You stop hoping because disappointment hurts. You stop praying honestly because silence feels too vulnerable. You stop dreaming because wanting something creates the possibility of grief. You stop naming desire because desire asks something of you.

You call it acceptance.

Sometimes it is.

Sometimes it is fear wearing maturity.

Fear does love a blazer and an air of emotional sophistication.

Fear loves a blazer. It can make staying small sound measured, wise, and emotionally mature when the more honest sentence is, "I am scared to want this much."

Emotional shrinking can look like numbness.

It can look like staying busy.

It can look like being "fine."

It can look like never asking for too much, never wanting too openly, never grieving too honestly, never celebrating too fully, never letting hope get large enough to hurt. The heart learns to stay small because small feels safer. Confidence cannot grow where desire, grief, hope, honesty, and courage are never allowed to take up space. This is why compassion with a spine has to hold both truths. Some lives shrink because the person is surviving something genuinely overwhelming. There are seasons where the goal is not expansion. It is stabilization. It is getting through the day, keeping the basics intact, resting, grieving, healing, recovering, and letting the body come back from what it has carried.

That matters. This book is not here to shame necessary contraction. There are times when life gets smaller because it has to. There are seasons where a smaller life is not avoidance.

It is wisdom.

It is recovery.

It is protection.

It is pacing.

It is the honest admission that the body, mind, heart, or spirit cannot expand yet. That should be respected. There is a difference between a season of stabilization and a pattern of avoidance.

Stabilization prepares for capacity.

Avoidance protects against it.

Stabilization says, "I need to gather strength before I expand."

Avoidance says, "I will call this limitation peace so I never have to test it."

Stabilization has a direction.

Avoidance has a hiding place.

Stabilization may move slowly, but it is still oriented toward restoration. Avoidance may look calm, but it is often organized around never returning to the thing that needs practice. Stabilization asks, “What support do I need so I can eventually re-enter life?” Avoidance asks, “How do I make sure I never have to feel that again?”

Telling the difference requires honesty.

It may also require support.

There are patterns people cannot always see clearly from inside themselves. A good therapist, supervisor, mentor, friend, partner, or trusted guide can help name the difference between rest and retreat, protection and avoidance, pacing and hiding.

Not everyone will do that well.

Some people will push too hard.

Some people will enable too much.

This is why the standard matters.

Compassion with a spine does not demand expansion without care. It also does not let care become a permanent excuse for contraction.

It asks, “What builds capacity here?”

That question belongs everywhere.

In therapy.

In supervision.

In leadership.

In parenting.

In friendship.

In faith.

In personal growth.

In the private places where you know whether you are resting or hiding. A shrinking life is not always a failed life.

Sometimes it is a protected life.

Sometimes it is a recovering life.

Sometimes it is a life waiting for enough steadiness to expand again. If shrinking becomes the pattern, confidence will suffer.

Confidence needs lived evidence.

It needs moments where you stayed.

Moments where you tried.

Moments where you repaired.

Moments where you spoke.

Moments where you entered the room unsure and left with proof that unsure did not mean incapable. Moments where you learned that discomfort could be carried without becoming the whole story. You cannot think your way into that evidence.

You practice your way into it.

That is the invitation at the end of Part I. Not to shame the ways you have shrunk. Not to deny the reasons avoidance made sense. Not to pretend language, diagnosis, validation, boundaries, and nervous-system awareness have no value. They do. The invitation is to ask whether those things are helping you grow, or helping you avoid growth with better words. Confidence is not built by making life as small as possible. It is built by expanding your capacity to meet life as it actually is.

Not all at once.

Not without support.

Not without fear.

One honest repetition at a time.

If shrinking can be practiced, expansion can be practiced, too. That is where Part II begins. With the belief that confidence is not a feeling you wait for. It is evidence you build. If your life has become smaller than your capacity, that does not mean you are broken. It means there is room to grow back.

Practice Point

Notice This

Where has your life become smaller in the name of comfort, peace, healing, or readiness? Look for patterns, not isolated choices.

Try This

Name one area where you want expansion. Choose one small action that creates evidence: one conversation, one task, one attempt, one step back into the room.

Measure This

Do not measure whether you felt confident. Measure whether you created evidence. Did your behavior move toward the life you want, even slightly? Confidence grows when your life gives it room.

PART II

What Actually Builds Confidence

Confidence is often misunderstood because it is marketed as a feeling.

Feel certain.

Feel powerful.

Feel magnetic.

Feel unstoppable.

Feel like the version of yourself who finally walks into every room without insecurity, doubt, comparison, body noise, fear, shame, or the persistent urge to disappear into a hoodie and become emotionally unavailable until further notice.

That version sounds nice.

It is also not real life.

Real confidence is not arrogance.

It is not constant certainty.

It is not emotional invulnerability.

It is not the absence of discomfort.

Real confidence is the practiced ability to remain with yourself while discomfort is present. That changes the whole conversation. If confidence is a feeling, you have to wait for it. If confidence is evidence, you can build it. This section moves from erosion to construction. Part I named the patterns that shrink capacity: language without practice, diagnosis without movement, avoidance disguised as healing, and the quiet cost of being treated as fragile.

Part II asks a different question: What actually helps people grow?

The answer is not more pressure without care.

It is not more self-criticism. It is not pretending that anxiety, trauma, grief, depression, burnout, learning differences, attention-related struggles, or relational wounds do not matter. They matter. They cannot be the only thing that matters. Growth requires a stronger kind of compassion; one that validates pain while still building capacity, that respects limits while still testing whether some limits can expand, that helps people stop organizing their lives around what feels easiest in the moment. If Part I asked where life has been shrinking, Part II asks what helps it widen again.

Confidence grows through repeated evidence.

Evidence grows through action.

Action often requires discomfort.

That means confidence is not something we talk ourselves into once and keep forever.

It is something we practice.

This section names the practices that build it.

Chapter 6: Confidence Is Not a Feeling; It Is Evidence

Most of us would prefer confidence to arrive before the risk.

We want it to show up early, prepared and reassuring, preferably with a clipboard, a timeline, and written confirmation that everything will go well. We want confidence before the application, before the conversation, before the boundary, before the gym, before the launch, before the first draft, before the apology, before the decision that might change something.

That would be lovely.

It is also not how confidence usually works.

Confidence is rarely the permission slip that lets you begin. More often, it is the receipt your life gives you after you practice beginning. It grows after you do the hard thing with your voice shaking, your body activated, your thoughts dramatic, and your internal commentary offering absolutely no useful customer service.

Then, over time, the body starts to believe what the behavior has been proving.

Confidence is annoying like that. It likes evidence more than potential.

Confidence is not what you feel before you do the hard thing. Most of the time, confidence is what grows after you survive doing it. This is inconvenient, of course, because most people would prefer confidence to arrive first. It would be lovely if confidence walked in before the application, the boundary, the presentation, the date, the difficult conversation, the gym, the launch, the apology, the decision, the interview, the first draft, the first attempt, and every other moment where we would rather have a signed certificate from the universe confirming that we will not embarrass ourselves. That is not how confidence usually works.

Preferably laminated, notarized, and delivered before we commit to anything emotionally risky.

Confidence is not built from certainty.

Annoying, I know. I also filed a complaint.

Confidence is not the same as self-esteem

Self-esteem often asks how you feel about yourself. Confidence asks what you trust yourself to practice. Those are related, but they are not identical. A person may have moments of decent self-esteem and still avoid anything that might expose them as inexperienced, imperfect, or still learning. Another person may feel uncertain, insecure, or unimpressive and still practice the next right thing with steadiness.

Self-esteem can be mood-dependent. If you only feel capable when you feel good about yourself, then every bad body day, awkward social moment, difficult conversation, or piece of feedback has the power to erase your confidence.

Practiced confidence is less fragile than that.

It does not require you to wake up feeling impressive. It asks whether you can keep one promise, take one step, ask one question, repair one mistake, or stay present long enough to give your nervous system new evidence.

This is why confidence can grow even during seasons where self-esteem feels inconsistent. You may not feel amazing. You may not feel magnetic. You may not feel certain. Every time your behavior aligns with your values despite those insecurities, confidence has something real to build from.

It is not built from personality, either. Some people may look confident because they are expressive, polished, charismatic, or comfortable being seen. That can be confidence, but it can also be performance, temperament, image management, or familiarity with being observed. The kind of confidence this book is building is deeper than presentation. It is the belief, practiced through experience, that you can meet a situation and remain with yourself inside it.

It is built from evidence.

You do something uncomfortable.

You survive it.

You learn from it.

You repeat it.

Your nervous system begins to collect proof.

I can do this.

I can recover from this.

I can tolerate this.

I can be new and still keep going.

I can feel unsure and still act.

I can make a mistake and still remain intact.

Confidence grows when your body has enough evidence that discomfort does not automatically mean danger, failure, rejection, collapse, or permanent humiliation. This is why affirmation alone is not enough.

Affirmations can help.

Words matter.

The way you speak to yourself can either steady you or sharpen the fear. A kind phrase can interrupt shame. A grounding sentence can create enough space to choose a different response. A reminder can help you take the next step. The body eventually asks for receipts. This is where affirmation and evidence must be distinguished.

The body is not trying to be difficult. It simply has a stricter reimbursement policy than the mind.

This book has been evidence for me. Not because I sat down feeling perfectly confident and author-like; absolutely not, and still not. There were plenty of moments where the page looked back at me like, "Are we doing this or just pretending with a laptop?" The confidence came through repetition: writing the sentence, revising the sentence, deleting the sentence that was trying too hard, coming back again, and watching the work become real because I kept showing up for it.

This book has exposed me in that exact way. I wanted the confidence before the pages. I wanted the certainty before the risk. Instead, the work kept requiring the same thing I am asking of you: one honest repetition before the feeling caught up.

Affirmation can steady.

Evidence strengthens.

Affirmation can interrupt the old sentence long enough for you to intentionally try something different. Evidence is what your life collects when you actually try. You may need the sentence, "I am capable," to help you begin. The sentence becomes sturdier when it is backed by lived proof: I did the thing. I stayed. I recovered. I tried again. Self-efficacy research has long emphasized the importance of mastery experiences: people build belief in their ability to act effectively through repeated experiences of doing, learning, adapting, and succeeding enough to trust themselves more (Bandura, 1977). That is why confidence cannot be reduced to positive self-talk.

Self-talk may open the door. Practice is what lets you walk through it. You can tell yourself, "I am capable," but if you repeatedly avoid every situation that would let you experience capability, the words will stay thin.

Not useless; thin.

Confidence thickens through lived evidence.

This is where many people get stuck. They wait to feel confident before they act, but action is what would build the confidence they are waiting for. So they remain in the waiting room of their own life.

The waiting room has terrible magazines.

Waiting to feel:

...ready.

...regulated.

...certain.

...healed enough.

...less anxious.

Waiting to feel more motivated.

Waiting until the timing is better, the body feels better, the mood is better, the plan is clearer, the risk is lower, the outcome is guaranteed, and the universe has finally stopped being rude and unpredictable.

Waiting can feel responsible.

Sometimes it is.

There are moments when preparation matters. Timing matters. Pacing matters. Safety matters. Support matters. Waiting becomes avoidance when it repeatedly delays the very practice that would build capacity. Confidence does not ask you to be fearless.

It asks you to create evidence.

Small evidence counts.

Evidence needs variety

Confidence also grows more sturdily when evidence comes from more than one area of life. If the only place you feel capable is work, then a relationship rupture may still make you feel powerless. If the only place you feel confident is caregiving, then being seen creatively may still feel terrifying. If the only place you feel steady is in private, then public visibility may still feel like a threat.

This is why repeated evidence matters across domains.

Body confidence may grow when you move your body while still feeling uncomfortable in it. Relational confidence may grow when you say the honest sentence and let the other person have their reaction. Professional confidence may grow when you ask for feedback and do not turn correction into proof that you are failing. Creative confidence may grow when you let imperfect work exist outside your head. Spiritual confidence may grow when you return to prayer, church, Scripture, silence, or community after a season where your faith felt thin.

The goal is not to become equally confident everywhere. That is not realistic. The goal is to become less dependent on avoidance everywhere. Every area where you practice creates a different kind of proof.

You begin to learn, "I can be uncomfortable in more than one room and still remain myself."

That is not loud confidence. It is portable confidence. The kind you can carry into new places because it is rooted in practice, not performance.

This matters because confidence does not always arrive through dramatic proof. Sometimes it grows through body confidence when you walk into the gym while still feeling exposed. Sometimes it grows through creative confidence when you post the imperfect thing and survive being seen. Sometimes it grows through relational confidence when you say the honest sentence before you have polished it into something painless. Sometimes it grows through professional confidence when you ask the question in the meeting instead of pretending you already know. Sometimes it grows through spiritual confidence when you return to prayer, community, worship, or quiet practice after a season where showing up felt hard.

Sometimes it grows through wellness when you start the routine imperfectly instead of waiting for the perfect plan.

Small evidence is still evidence.

Tiny receipts still count when the body is learning how to trust you again.

Opening the email counts.

Making the appointment counts.

Going to the class counts.

Asking the question counts.

Saying, “I need to think about that,” instead of automatically saying yes counts.

Trying the thing badly counts.

Returning after a setback counts.

Staying in the conversation thirty seconds longer than usual counts.

Taking the walk counts.

Writing the first ugly sentence counts.

Doing the boring foundational thing that nobody will clap for counts. Confidence is less glamorous than people want it to be. There are a few myths worth naming here.

Myth: confident people do not feel fear. Reality: Many do. They have simply practiced moving with fear present.

Myth: confidence comes before action. Reality: Often, it follows action. Myth: confidence means everyone approves. Reality: Real confidence can tolerate disapproval without collapsing into self-abandonment.

Myth: confidence is a personality trait. Reality: Some people are naturally more outgoing, but practiced confidence is built through evidence.

Myth: confidence means never needing support. Reality: Mature confidence knows when support is needed and uses it without turning support into avoidance.

These myths matter because if you believe confidence should feel effortless, you may miss the moments where confidence is actually being built. It is built in repetition. This is one of the reasons social media confidence can be so misleading. Confidence is often shown as the reveal: the polished outfit, the transformation photo, the launch announcement, the strong caption, the healed version, the person finally glowing in good lighting and apparently no longer bothered by human nonsense.

Confidence is usually built before the reveal.

In the awkward middle. In the attempt that no one saw. In the boundary that made your stomach hurt. In the gym session where you felt uncomfortable in your body and went anyway. In the conversation where your voice shook.

In the draft that was messy. In the meeting where you spoke before you felt fully ready. In the moment where you wanted to disappear but chose to stay present.

That is where confidence grows.

Not in the performance of being unbothered, but in the practice of being willing.

This matters clinically, too.

In therapy, confidence often grows through behavioral evidence. A client with anxiety does not become confident by intellectually understanding anxiety alone. They become more confident when they repeatedly experience anxiety rising and falling without avoidance controlling the outcome. A client working on boundaries does not become confident because they wrote a beautiful script in session. They become more confident when they use the boundary, tolerate the reaction, and survive the discomfort that follows. A client with depression does not wait until motivation appears perfectly. They often begin with small behavioral activation steps that create movement before mood improves.

A student does not become clinically confident by reading every theory until uncertainty disappears. They become more confident through supervised practice, feedback, mistakes, repair, and repetition. Confidence is not a precondition for growth. It is often a result of growth itself.

That means the question shifts. Instead of asking, "Do I feel confident?" ask, "What evidence am I building?" Instead of asking, "Do I feel ready?" ask, "What is the next honest repetition?" Instead of asking, "Can I guarantee this will go well?" ask, "Can I practice showing up with support, humility, and willingness?"

This shift is not harsh.

It is freeing.

If confidence is a feeling, then you are at the mercy of whether the feeling arrives. If confidence is evidence, then you can participate in building it.

You can choose the next repetition.

You can create the next proof point.

You can stop waiting for your nervous system to hand you certainty before you begin. This does not mean forcing yourself into everything.

It does not mean ignoring limits. It does not mean mistaking overwhelm for growth. It means learning to tell the difference between a stop sign and a stretch point.

Some things are unsafe.

Some things are unwise.

Some things require pacing, support, treatment, supervision, consultation, rest, or protection. Some things are simply uncomfortable because they matter. Confidence grows when you learn the difference.

Not perfectly.

Not all at once.

Through practice.

The goal is not to become someone who never feels uncertain. The goal is to become someone who no longer treats uncertainty as proof that they are incapable. That is a different kind of confidence.

Quieter.

Sturdier.

Less performative.

More honest.

The kind that can say, "I am scared, and I am still here." The kind that can say, "I do not feel ready, and I can take one step." The kind that can say, "This is uncomfortable, and discomfort is not the same as danger." The kind that grows because you gave it evidence.

Not once.

Repeatedly.

Practice Point

Notice This

Where are you waiting to feel confident before you act? Pay attention to places where readiness has become the requirement for movement.

Try This

Choose one small action that would create evidence. Make it specific and doable: send the email, ask the question, start the task, attend the class, write the first paragraph, say the first honest sentence.

Measure This

Do not measure whether you felt confident. Measure whether you created proof. Did you take action while discomfort was present? Confidence grows when your life gives your nervous system evidence.

Chapter 7: Discomfort Is Not the Enemy

Discomfort is not proof that something has gone wrong. Sometimes discomfort is proof that something important is happening. This is one of the hardest lessons to learn in a culture that has become increasingly skilled at tracking, naming, analyzing, and avoiding uncomfortable internal states.

We notice anxiety.

We notice tension.

We notice activation.

We notice dread.

We notice insecurity.

We notice shame.

We notice the stomach drop, the tight chest, the racing thoughts, the heat in the face, the urge to explain, escape, shut down, scroll, snack, cancel, apologize, overfunction, or become a deeply unavailable houseplant.

Noticing matters.

Awareness matters.

The problem begins when every uncomfortable sensation is treated as instruction.

Discomfort says, “Pay attention.”

It does not always say, “Stop.”

Sometimes it says, “Please ask a better question before handing me the keys.”

I have had plenty of moments where discomfort showed up so convincingly that it deserved an Oscar and possibly a small legal team. Posting something direct. Having a hard conversation. Walking into a room where I was still becoming the version of myself the room required. My body did not always feel calm. That did not automatically mean I was unsafe. Sometimes it meant I was doing something honest before it felt familiar.

I do not always meet discomfort with serene maturity and a warm cup of tea. Sometimes I meet it with a dramatic inner monologue, tight shoulders, and the deep suspicion that growth has poor timing. The practice is not pretending otherwise. The practice is staying connected anyway.

That pause is one of the foundations of capacity. A racing heart before public speaking may mean the body is preparing for performance. A wave of guilt after setting a boundary may mean you are interrupting an old pattern. Anxiety before exposure may mean you are approaching something your nervous system has been trained to avoid. Sadness during change may mean you are grieving what is ending, not necessarily that the change is wrong. Shame after feedback may mean you care about doing well, not that you are being harmed.

Discomfort is information.

It may be loud, but loud is not the same as accurate.

Some feelings arrive with a siren and a PowerPoint. That still does not make them the board of directors.

Discomfort versus danger

Discomfort and danger cannot be treated as synonyms. Danger requires protection. Discomfort requires discernment, support, and often practice.

The challenge is that both can feel urgent. A boundary conversation may make your stomach drop. So can an unsafe situation. Feedback may make your face hot. So can humiliation. Trying something new may create a racing heart. So can real threat. The body gives information, but it does not always give interpretation.

This is why wisdom matters.

If the situation is unsafe, the answer is not exposure. It is protection, support, intervention, distance, reporting, safety planning, or whatever care the situation requires. If the situation is safe and the distress is coming from unfamiliarity, shame, old learning, fear of disappointment, or the discomfort of growth, the answer may not be escape. The answer may be a supported next step.

Discernment is not weakness. It is not overthinking. It is the practice of refusing both extremes: ignoring the body completely or treating every alarm as absolute truth.

It is not always authority.

When discomfort becomes authority, it begins making decisions.

Do not go.

Do not ask.

Do not say it.

Do not try.

Do not risk.

Do not feel.

Do not continue.

Do not find out.

Life begins to organize around internal weather. The problem is that internal weather changes constantly. If every emotional storm determines the direction of your life, your life will become reactive instead of rooted.

This does not mean ignoring discomfort.

Ignoring discomfort is not strength.

It is usually just another form of disconnection. Compassion with a spine is not about pushing through everything while pretending your body is not speaking. It is about listening carefully without automatically obeying fear.

There is a difference.

Listening asks, “What is happening here?”

Obeying says, “This feeling gets to decide.”

Listening creates space.

Obeying collapses choice.

The more a person practices pausing between feeling and action, the more capacity begins to grow.

That pause can be small.

One breath.

One sentence.

One moment of naming what is happening.

"This is anxiety."

"This is shame."

"This is fear of conflict."

"This is old guilt."

"This is discomfort, not danger."

"This is hard, and I do not have to decide from urgency." That pause matters because urgency is often where avoidance hides.

Urgency says, "Fix this now."

"Escape now."

"Answer now."

"Explain now."

"Cancel now."

"Make the feeling stop now."

Many feelings do not need to be fixed immediately. They need to be tolerated long enough to pass through the body without taking over the steering wheel.

This is distress tolerance.

Not the romanticized kind.

Not the internet version that makes it sound like you can breathe once, drink water, light a candle, and become a regulated woodland creature. Real distress tolerance is less cute. It is the practiced ability to remain present with discomfort without immediately escaping, numbing, attacking, collapsing, or handing the feeling control of your behavior (Linehan, 2015).

No one has ever looked especially aesthetic practicing distress tolerance in real time. That is fine. The goal is capacity, not content.

There is usually no aesthetic candle involved, and frankly that feels rude.

It is staying in the room.

It is not sending the defensive text.

It is letting the anxiety rise while you open the email anyway. It is feeling the embarrassment and still repairing. It is noticing the urge to quit and choosing to take one smaller step instead. It is allowing guilt to exist after a boundary without treating guilt as evidence that the boundary was wrong. Distress tolerance builds confidence because it teaches the body, "I can feel this and remain intact." That is powerful evidence. Most people do not need to become less emotional. They need more practice staying with emotion. There is a difference between feeling deeply and being ruled by feeling.

Feeling deeply is human.

Being ruled by feeling is exhausting.

When people do not have tolerance for discomfort, life becomes organized around preventing it. They may need constant reassurance. They may avoid honest conversations. They may interpret delayed responses as rejection. They may over-explain every boundary. They may avoid opportunities that could build competence. They may become dependent on other people managing the emotional temperature around them. This is not because they are bad. It is because they have not yet built enough confidence in their ability to experience discomfort and remain steady.

That confidence can be built.

It requires practice.

Not dramatic practice.

Repeated practice.

Small moments of staying.

Small moments of engaging.

Small moments of not obeying the first escape impulse. Small moments of letting the feeling be present without letting it become the whole room. The point is not to love discomfort. No one needs to become spiritually enthusiastic about awkward conversations, feedback, exposure, grief, rejection, uncertainty, or the special kind of personal development that occurs when technology fails five minutes before you need to look competent.

Discomfort is still uncomfortable. The point is not to worship it. The point is to stop fearing it so much that it runs your life. Growth often requires discomfort because growth requires contact with what is not yet familiar.

Learning is uncomfortable.

Repair is uncomfortable.

Boundaries are uncomfortable.

Accountability is uncomfortable.

Intimacy is uncomfortable.

Leadership is uncomfortable.

Healing is uncomfortable.

Confidence is uncomfortable before it becomes familiar. That is why comfort cannot be the only metric. Comfort tells you what feels easy. It does not always tell you what is healthy. It does not always tell you what is honest. It does not always tell you what will build capacity. This is where many people confuse peace with avoidance. Peace is not the absence of all discomfort. Sometimes peace is what becomes possible after honesty.

Sometimes peace comes after the boundary.

After the hard conversation.

After the decision.

After the apology.

After the action you were avoiding.

Avoidance often creates short-term calm and long-term tension. Growth often creates short-term discomfort and long-term freedom.

The timing matters. If you only measure the moment, avoidance looks better. If you measure the pattern, growth tells the truth. This is especially important for people who are trying to rebuild confidence. A person may think, "I will become confident when I stop feeling anxious." Confidence is often built by learning anxiety can come along without being in charge. A person may think, "I will become confident when criticism no longer hurts." Confidence is often built by learning that feedback can sting and still be useful. A person may think, "I will become confident when boundaries feel easy." Confidence is often built by setting boundaries while they still feel uncomfortable.

A person may think, "I will become confident when I am no longer afraid to be seen." Confidence is often built by allowing yourself to be seen before fear fully leaves.

Discomfort is not the enemy.

Avoidance is the teacher we have to question.

It has had the microphone long enough.

Sometimes discomfort is a warning.

Sometimes it is a wound.

Sometimes it is a signal that something needs attention. Sometimes it is old learning being activated by new growth. Sometimes it is the body reacting to expansion.

Wisdom is learning the difference. That wisdom does not come from treating every feeling as fact. It comes from curiosity, support, practice, and discernment.

Ask better questions.

Questions to ask discomfort

When discomfort rises, the goal is not to interrogate yourself into numbness. The goal is to create enough space to choose.

Ask: What are you trying to protect me from?

Ask: Is this danger, or unfamiliarity?

Ask: Is this harmful, or humbling?

Ask: Is this my current reality, or an old alarm entering a new room?

Ask: What would avoidance teach me if I obeyed it right now?

Ask: What would practice teach me if I stayed connected to my values?

Ask: What support would make the next step wise rather than reckless?

These questions slow the automatic loop. They interrupt the assumption that urgency equals truth. They also help prevent the opposite error: pushing through something that actually requires protection, rest, or support.

This is why discomfort tolerance is not the same as force. Force says, "Ignore the feeling." Avoidance says, "Obey the feeling." Capacity says, "Listen, assess, and choose."

That middle path is not always neat. It requires repetition. It requires humility. It requires being willing to admit that fear may be loud without being accurate, and that courage may be quiet without being absent.

When discomfort shows up, ask it better questions before you hand it the decision. What are you trying to protect me from? Is this danger, or is this unfamiliarity? Is this an old alarm responding to a new situation?

What would avoidance teach me here?

What would practice teach me here?

What action would align with my values, not just my urge for relief? Those questions create enough space for choice, which is central to values-based approaches to change (Hayes et al., 2012).

Is this unsafe, or unfamiliar?

Is this harmful, or humbling?

Is this boundary wrong, or am I uncomfortable with someone being disappointed? Is this feedback cruel, or am I activated by correction? Is this opportunity misaligned, or am I scared of being new?

Is this rest, or retreat?

Is this peace, or avoidance with better branding?

These questions are not always easy.

They are useful.

They return choice to the person. That is where confidence grows: in the space between feeling and action. Not because discomfort disappears. The person learns they do not have to disappear when discomfort arrives.

Practice Point

Notice This

Pay attention to the feelings you treat as automatic stop signs. Is it anxiety, guilt, shame, uncertainty, awkwardness, disappointment, or fear of being misunderstood?

Try This

The next time discomfort rises, pause before acting. Name the feeling, then ask: "Is this unsafe, or is this uncomfortable?" Choose one response from steadiness instead of urgency.

Measure This

Track whether you created space between feeling and action. Did you pause? Did you choose? Did you stay connected to your values instead of obeying the first escape impulse?

Chapter 8: Self-Regulation and Distress Tolerance

Self-regulation is not the ability to stay calm all the time.

That would be convenient.

It would also be suspicious.

No one is that calm without either deep practice or a secret lair.

A fully calm human in every circumstance is either deeply practiced, deeply disconnected, or waiting to surprise everyone in Chapter 12. Real self-regulation is not constant calm. Self-regulation, in this framework, means the ability to notice internal experience and respond with enough steadiness to choose your next action. Distress tolerance means the ability to experience discomfort without immediately escaping, attacking, numbing, collapsing, or making the feeling the only authority in the room. Emotional intensity is the volume of the feeling. Urgency is the pressure to act immediately so the feeling will stop. Coping is any strategy used to respond to distress.

Either way, I have follow-up questions.

Several, actually.

Regulation that returns you to life

A regulation strategy has to be measured by what it helps you return to. If breathing helps you stay in the conversation with more steadiness, it is serving growth. If grounding helps you open the email instead of avoiding it for another week, it is serving capacity. If taking a pause helps you come back and repair, it is serving emotional adulthood.

If a strategy only lowers distress while helping you exit the work every time discomfort appears, then it may be functioning as avoidance with better language.

This does not make the strategy bad. It means the function needs to be examined.

A walk can be regulation, or it can be escape. A break can be wise, or it can become disappearance. Silence can be restraint, or it can be avoidance. Asking for reassurance can be human, or it can become a loop that prevents self-trust. The behavior alone does not tell the whole story. The function tells the truth.

Regulation should help you re-enter life with more choice. It should not become a ritual that life has to wait for indefinitely. Sometimes the most regulated next step is not feeling calm. Sometimes it is doing the value-aligned thing while your body is still catching up.

Avoidance is coping that protects relief at the expense of capacity. Those definitions matter because emotion regulation and distress tolerance are not only about reducing intensity; they are also about restoring choice and effective action (Gross, 1998; Linehan, 2015). It is the ability to notice what is happening inside you and respond with enough steadiness to remain connected to your values, choices, and responsibilities.

Sometimes regulation looks calm.

Sometimes it looks like slowing down.

Sometimes it looks like taking a breath before answering. Sometimes it looks like stepping away for ten minutes so you do not say the thing your nervous system drafted with absolutely no legal review. Sometimes it looks like asking for support. Sometimes it looks like staying in the room. Sometimes it looks like doing the task while anxious. Sometimes it looks like letting yourself cry without deciding the whole day is ruined. Self-regulation is not about becoming emotionless. It is about becoming less controlled by emotional intensity. This is important because I am not someone who believes emotional strength means becoming unreadable. I have feelings. I have facial expressions that occasionally file their own reports before I have approved them. Regulation has not meant becoming less human; it has meant learning to pause long enough that my values get a vote before my intensity writes the whole script. That matters because emotional intensity is persuasive. When anxiety is loud, avoidance feels logical. When shame is loud, hiding feels necessary.

Some days that pause is elegant. Some days it is held together by water, prayer, a walk, and the decision not to let my first reaction become a public document.

Mine has absolutely sent emails to committee without my consent.

When anger is loud, attack feels justified. When sadness is loud, withdrawal feels permanent. When guilt is loud, over-explaining feels responsible. When fear is loud, control feels like safety.

Intensity makes feelings sound like facts.

Self-regulation helps create enough space to question them.

Not dismiss them.

Question them.

This is one of the differences between compassion and indulgence. Compassion says, "This feeling makes sense, and we still need to choose well." Indulgence says, "This feeling makes sense, so it gets to run the room." A lot of people mistake the second one for kindness.

It is not. Letting every emotion dictate behavior does not honor the emotion. It gives the emotion a job it was never meant to hold.

Emotions are signals.

They are not always strategies. Anger may signal that something feels unjust. It does not automatically know how to have a repair conversation.

Anxiety may signal uncertainty.

It does not automatically know what is safe.

Shame may signal fear of disconnection. It does not automatically know whether you have done something wrong. Guilt may signal a value conflict.

It does not automatically mean you are responsible for someone else's feelings. Self-regulation allows you to hear the signal without becoming trapped inside it.

That ability is practiced.

It is not built through one coping skill.

Regulation in relationship with responsibility

Self-regulation becomes more mature when it remains connected to responsibility. It is not only about what happens inside the body. It is also about what happens next in the relationship, the work, the task, or the commitment.

If you calm down but never return to the conversation, regulation has become exit. If you journal every feeling but never name the boundary, insight has become delay. If you breathe through the urge to respond but still punish someone with silence for three days, calm has not become responsibility. If you understand why you were activated but refuse to repair your impact, awareness has not become growth.

This is not meant to shame the need for pause. Pausing can be wise. It can prevent harm. It can help the body settle enough to choose more clearly.

A pause has integrity when it remains connected to return.

That is why one of the most important regulated sentences is, "I need a minute, and I will come back."

The "I need a minute" honors the body.

The "I will come back" protects the relationship, the responsibility, and the work.

Both matter.

It is not built by saving a graphic about the nervous system and then continuing to live like every uncomfortable feeling is an emergency. It is not built by waiting until life stops being stressful. It is built in the actual moments where activation shows up and you choose what to practice next. This is where distress tolerance becomes essential. Distress tolerance is the bridge between feeling and functioning. Without distress tolerance, people often become dependent on immediate relief. They need the anxiety to drop before they act. They need the guilt to disappear before they hold the boundary. They need the confidence to arrive before they begin.

They need the shame to quiet before they repair.

They need motivation before they move.

They need certainty before they decide.

Distress tolerance teaches a different order.

Act with anxiety present.

Hold the boundary with guilt present.

Begin with uncertainty present.

Repair with shame present.

Move before motivation arrives.

Decide without perfect certainty.

This does not mean being reckless.

It means learning that discomfort does not have to be resolved before life can be lived. A person who cannot tolerate distress will often organize their life around immediate emotional relief. A person who can tolerate distress has more choices. That is the point. Regulation is not about making feelings smaller so life can finally begin. It is about increasing capacity so feelings do not keep ending the attempt. There are many ways to practice regulation.

The skill is not the point; the direction is

People can become very skilled at collecting coping tools and still avoid change. They can know breathing techniques, grounding exercises, cognitive reframes, sensory strategies, journaling prompts, and communication scripts, yet still use them primarily to avoid the task, the boundary, the repair, the exposure, or the responsibility waiting on the other side.

The point of a skill is not that it sounds therapeutic. The point is where it takes you.

A body-based skill may help you settle enough to stay. A cognitive skill may help you separate feeling from fact. A relational skill may help you ask for support without making someone else responsible for your whole internal world. A behavioral skill may help you move before motivation appears. A values-based skill may help you choose integrity over immediate relief (Hayes et al., 2012).

Each one can be useful. Each one can also be misused.

This is why the question has to stay active: "Is this helping me re-enter what matters, or is it helping me avoid it?"

That question does not shame coping. It restores purpose to it.

Some are physical.

Slow your breathing.

Unclench your jaw.

Feel your feet on the floor.

Take a short walk.

Drink water.

Orient to the room.

Lower your shoulders.

Name five things you see.

Use temperature, movement, or pressure to help the body come back into the present.

Some are cognitive.

Name the emotion.

Identify the urge.

Separate feeling from fact.

Ask what story your nervous system is telling.

Look for the next effective action.

Remind yourself, "This is uncomfortable, not unmanageable."

Some are relational.

Ask for support.

Tell the truth without making someone else responsible for fixing the feeling.

Request a pause.

Return to the conversation.

Repair when you miss the mark.

Allow someone safe to sit with you without handing them the steering wheel.

Some are behavioral.

Some are values-based.

Ask what matters here.

Ask what kind of person you are trying to become in this moment. Ask what action protects your integrity, not just your comfort. Ask what would move you toward the life you are building rather than away from the feeling you dislike. Values-based regulation does not always make the feeling smaller.

It makes the next step clearer.

Do the next small task.

Complete the thing you are avoiding.

Stay in the room.

Follow through.

Practice the boundary.

Take the exposure step.

Choose the value-based action even while the feeling is still present. The method matters less than the function. Does the strategy help you return to choice?

Regulation should not become a waiting room

Many people start using regulation skills because they want to feel better before they act. That is understandable. No one wants to enter the hard conversation, the task, the repair, the meeting, or the exposure while their body is still activated. Regulation is not meant to become an endless waiting room where life stands outside the door until calm finally arrives.

Sometimes calm will not arrive before the next step. Sometimes the next step is what teaches calm that it is safe to return.

This is where distress tolerance becomes more important than perfect regulation. You may breathe and still feel anxious. You may ground and still feel embarrassed. You may take a walk and still need to have the conversation. You may journal and still need to apologize. You may pray and still need to act.

A skill has done its job when it helps you return to choice, not when it guarantees comfort.

That is a very different standard. It allows care without letting care become a reason to stay outside your life.

This becomes the coping skill test.

Does this return me to choice?

Does this support functioning?

Does this build capacity?

Does this align with my values?

Does this help me re-enter life?

Or does it simply help me avoid?

That test keeps self-regulation connected to growth. Does it help you stay connected to your values?

Does it help you act effectively?

Does it build capacity over time?

Or does it simply help you escape? A coping skill is not automatically healthy because it lowers distress.

Avoidance lowers distress, too.

Numbing lowers distress.

Over-reassurance lowers distress.

Control lowers distress.

Canceling everything lowers distress.

The question is not only, “Did this make me feel better?”

The question is, “Did this help me become more capable?”

That is the part coping-skills influencers forget to put on the slide.

That question is the spine.

Tiny sentence. Whole backbone.

Not the vibes. Not the font choice. The question.

It is deeply unglamorous. It is also where most of the actual work lives.

Without it, self-regulation becomes another way to avoid. People can become so focused on calming their nervous system that they forget the nervous system is also built to mobilize.

Activation is not always a malfunction.

Sometimes activation is preparation.

The body activates for challenge.

For performance.

For conflict.

For risk.

For intimacy.

For grief.

For change.

For growth.

The goal is not to erase activation. The goal is to build a relationship with it. To be able to say, "My body is activated, and I can still choose."

That sentence is confidence in motion.

Not perfect confidence.

Practiced confidence.

When you can tolerate distress, your life gets larger.

You can have harder conversations.

You can receive feedback without collapsing.

You can set boundaries without needing everyone to like them.

You can try new things without requiring immediate excellence.

You can feel grief without becoming hopeless.

You can feel anxiety without becoming avoidant.

You can feel shame without hiding forever.

You can feel anger without becoming destructive.

This is emotional strength.

Not emotional numbness.

Emotional strength is not the absence of feeling. It is the ability to stay connected to yourself while feeling. That is what many people are actually seeking when they say they want confidence. They do not only want to feel good in a room. They want to trust that they can handle themselves in the room. They want to know they can survive discomfort, conflict, uncertainty, disappointment, and being seen. They want evidence that they will not abandon themselves the moment things become hard. Self-regulation and distress tolerance build that evidence.

Not because they make life painless.

They make life more livable.

You do not need to become calm enough to begin. You need to become steady enough to practice.

Practice Point

Notice This

What do you usually do when distress rises? Do you escape, explain, shut down, control, numb, attack, overfunction, seek reassurance, or freeze?

Try This

Choose one regulation strategy that returns you to choice instead of escape. Use it in a real moment of discomfort, then take one small value-based action.

Measure This

Ask: did this strategy help me avoid life, or re-enter it? Distress tolerance grows when regulation supports action, not when it becomes another form of retreat.

Chapter 9: Boundaries That Build Trust

A boundary is not only a wall.

That is one of the reasons people misunderstand it. They imagine boundaries as something cold, hard, defensive, and closed. A boundary becomes the thing that keeps people out, ends conversations, protects peace, and proves someone is finally done being available.

Sometimes boundaries do protect. Sometimes they need to.

However, a healthy boundary is also a structure. It is the fence around the garden, not because the garden hates people, but because something living needs a defined space to grow. It is the railing on the stairs, not because stairs are bad, but because movement needs support. It is the frame of a house, not because openness is wrong, but because without structure, nothing stands for very long.

A boundary tells the truth about where care can happen without resentment taking over the room.

A boundary is not proof that love failed. Sometimes it is the first thing giving love a place to stand.

Boundaries are often described as protection.

That is true.

It is also incomplete.

Boundaries do not only protect you.

They reveal you.

They reveal what you value.

What you will participate in.

What you will no longer normalize.

What you are responsible for.

What you are not responsible for.

What kind of relationship can actually exist without resentment quietly doing drywall damage behind the scenes. A boundary is not just a wall.

It is a structure. Structures are not built only to keep things out. They are built to help something stand. This matters because boundary language has become everywhere. People talk about boundaries in therapy, online, at work, in friendships, in dating, in families, in comment sections, in captions, and sometimes in ways that make the word boundary sound less like a relational practice and more like a decorative weapon.

Preferably posted over a neutral background with a very serious font.

"I am setting a boundary" can mean many things now.

Sometimes it means, "I am finally naming a real limit."

Sometimes it means, "I am trying to control your response."

Sometimes it means, "I do not want to feel uncomfortable."

Sometimes it means, "I am ending the conversation without having to tolerate disagreement."

Sometimes it means, "I am protecting my peace." Sometimes it means, "I am avoiding accountability but using therapeutic language so it looks evolved." This is why precision matters. A boundary, a request, and a control attempt are not the same thing. A request says, "Here is what I am asking from you."

Boundaries in actual settings

The difference gets clearer in real life. In a family, a request may sound like, "Please do not comment on my body." A boundary may sound like, "If my body becomes the topic, I am going to leave the conversation." A control attempt may sound like, "You are not allowed to have any thoughts about my body because I do not want to feel uncomfortable."

At work, a request may be, "Please give me notice before adding a new task." A boundary may be, "I cannot complete this by Friday unless another priority is moved." A control attempt may be, "No one can ever ask me for something urgent because urgency activates me."

In relationships, a request may be, "I would like more communication when plans change." A boundary may be, "If plans repeatedly change without communication, I am going to stop arranging my day around them." A control attempt may be, "You have to respond exactly the way I need so I never feel anxious."

The language can look similar at first. The responsibility is different.

Requests invite. Boundaries clarify. Control attempts demand emotional safety through someone else's compliance.

That is why precision matters. Without it, people may call control a boundary and then wonder why the relationship becomes more tense instead of more honest.

A boundary says, "Here is what I will do." A control attempt says, "Here is what you must do so I never have to feel uncomfortable."

Requests are allowed.

Boundaries are necessary.

Control attempts should be named honestly.

When people confuse these, boundary language becomes blurry fast. A boundary is about your behavior. It is not a demand that someone else never disappoint, frustrate, misunderstand, disagree with, challenge, or inconvenience you.

A boundary says, "Here is what I will do." A control attempt says, "Here is what you must do so I never feel uncomfortable."

Those are not the same thing.

A boundary may sound like:

Boundaries may show up in family systems when you stop absorbing every emotional crisis. They may show up in romantic relationships when you name what you need instead of hoping resentment will translate. They may show up at work when you clarify availability, role, scope, or deadline. They may show up online when you stop giving strangers access to your nervous system through every comment, message, or notification. They may show up around emotional labor when you stop becoming everyone's processing center. They may show up around body comments when you decide your body is not a group discussion. They may show up around time when you stop treating availability as proof of love.

Different settings.

Same structure.

A boundary clarifies what you will participate in and what you will do next. "I cannot continue this conversation if yelling continues, so I am going to take a break and come back when we can speak respectfully." "I am not available to answer work messages after hours unless it is urgent."

"I am not discussing my body." "I can help with this for thirty minutes, but I cannot take over the whole task." "I am willing to talk about the issue, but I am not willing to be insulted."

"I need more notice before committing."

"I am going to follow through with what I said."

A boundary is clear.

It is specific.

It is connected to action.

It does not require the other person to like it in order for it to be real.

This is where boundaries build confidence.

Not when they are written perfectly.

Not when they are received warmly.

Not when everyone claps and says, "Thank you for your clear communication. I respect your growth and will adjust accordingly."

That would be nice. It is also not the standard human setting. Boundaries build confidence when you tolerate what happens after you set them.

Human beings are usually running the beta version.

Disappointment.

Pushback.

Silence.

Misunderstanding.

Tension.

Guilt.

Second-guessing.

The urge to soften, over-explain, or immediately make the other person comfortable. The hardest part of a boundary is often not naming it, but surviving the emotional aftermath without abandoning yourself. I have had boundaries that felt clear in my head and wildly inconvenient once another human had a reaction to them. That is usually where the real work begins. Not in drafting the sentence. I can draft a sentence. I can draft seventeen versions of a sentence and then have opinions about the punctuation. The harder part is not turning the boundary into a group project the moment guilt shows up.

This one still humbles me. I can know the boundary is right and still feel the old urge to soften it until everyone else is comfortable and I am somehow responsible for the emotional weather again.

I say this as someone who respects both clarity and a well-organized exhibit list more than I should.

This is why boundaries require capacity. Boundaries often feel bad before they feel healthy. They may activate guilt if you were taught to be easy. They may activate fear if you were taught conflict means abandonment. They may activate shame if you were taught needs make you selfish. They may activate panic if someone else has always been allowed to punish your limits. They may activate grief because the boundary reveals how long you went without one. That discomfort does not automatically mean the boundary is wrong. Sometimes it means the boundary is new. If you cannot tolerate guilt, your boundary will collapse when someone is disappointed. If you cannot tolerate conflict, your boundary will soften when someone pushes back.

Why boundaries feel bad

Boundaries feel bad for many people because the body remembers what limits used to cost. If a limit was punished, a boundary may feel dangerous. If disagreement led to withdrawal, a boundary may feel like abandonment. If love was tied to usefulness, a boundary may feel selfish. If peace depended on silence, a boundary may feel disruptive.

That discomfort deserves compassion.

It also deserves interpretation.

A boundary may feel wrong because it is wrong. That is possible. Boundaries can be rigid, reactive, unclear, or punitive. A boundary may also feel wrong because it is interrupting an old role.

The fixer feels guilty when they stop fixing.

The peacekeeper feels cruel when they stop smoothing everything over.

The overfunctioner feels irresponsible when they stop carrying what belongs to someone else.

The invisible one feels exposed when they finally say what they need.

That discomfort is not proof that the boundary failed. It may be proof that the boundary is asking an old identity to loosen its grip.

This is why boundaries require follow-through, not just language. The sentence matters, but the confidence comes from what happens after the sentence.

If you cannot tolerate being misunderstood, your boundary will turn into a twenty-seven-minute closing argument with exhibits, citations, and a level of intensity that suggests you are trying to convince both them and yourself. If you cannot tolerate someone not liking your limit, you may keep calling it communication while actually negotiating against yourself. Boundaries are not effective because they prevent discomfort. They are effective because they clarify responsibility. You are responsible for communicating your limit.

You are responsible for following through.

You are responsible for managing your discomfort after the boundary is set. You are responsible for repair if you communicate poorly. You are not responsible for making the other person happy about the limit. You are not responsible for preventing all disappointment. You are not responsible for controlling whether they agree. Trust starts there. Trust in yourself grows when your words and actions match: when you say no and do not immediately turn it into yes because someone sighed; when you say you need time and actually take it; when you say you are unavailable and stop performing availability; when you say something matters and then act like it matters.

Self-trust is built through follow-through.

This is deeply inconvenient for those of us who prefer the draft version of courage.

Follow-through is where boundaries become real

Many people think the power of a boundary is in the wording. Wording matters. Clarity matters. Tone matters. The power of a boundary is in the follow-through.

A boundary without follow-through becomes a suggestion. A repeated boundary without action becomes an announcement that the pattern can continue. This is why people often feel increasingly frustrated after they "set a boundary" several times and nothing changes. They may have stated a preference. They may have made a request. They may even have named a limit. If their behavior never changes when the limit is crossed, the boundary has not become structure yet.

This is not about being punitive. It is about making words and actions match.

If you say you cannot discuss your body and then remain in every conversation where your body is discussed, the other person may learn that the discomfort is tolerable for you even when the words say it is not. If you say you are unavailable after work and then answer every nonurgent message, the system learns your stated boundary is negotiable. If you say yelling ends the conversation and then stay through yelling every time, the pattern remains intact.

Follow-through teaches your life that your limits are real.

That is why boundaries build self-trust. They show you that you can tell the truth and then act like it matters.

Relational trust is built through clarity. People may not always like your boundaries, but unclear relationships usually create more damage over time than honest ones.

When boundaries are avoided, resentment grows. When boundaries are over-explained, they become unstable. When boundaries are weaponized, they become control. When boundaries are held with steadiness, relationships become clearer.

Clear does not always mean comfortable.

Clear means honest.

That honesty can strengthen relationships that are capable of growth. It can also reveal relationships that were dependent on your lack of boundaries.

That part is painful.

It is also useful. Some relationships feel peaceful only because one person is over-accommodating. Some families function only because certain people never say no. Some workplaces feel smooth only because someone is absorbing unreasonable expectations. Some friendships remain easy only because conflict never gets addressed.

Boundaries disrupt those patterns.

That disruption is not automatically harm.

Sometimes it is the first honest thing that has happened in a long time. This is where Growing with Confidence meets Compassion with a Spine again. Confidence does not grow from being liked by everyone. It grows from being able to remain connected to your values even when approval is not guaranteed. Compassion does not mean abandoning your limits so others never feel uncomfortable. A spine does not mean becoming cold, rigid, or punitive. It means you can be kind without being endlessly available.

You can be loving without being absorbent.

You can be accountable without being controlled.

You can be generous without abandoning yourself.

You can tolerate the tension that clarity creates.

That is a skill.

Like every skill in this book, it is practiced. Start small. A real boundary does not have to be dramatic. You do not need to announce your entire healing era with cinematic lighting and a soundtrack.

The cinematic lighting is optional; the follow-through is not.

You can begin with one honest sentence.

"I cannot commit to that."

"I need to check my schedule before I answer."

"I am not available for that conversation right now."

"I hear you, and my answer is still no."

"I am willing to talk, but not if we are yelling."

"I need to leave by six."

"I am not taking responsibility for that."

Then follow through.

That is where the confidence builds.

In the follow-through.

In the moment after the sentence.

In the guilt.

In the silence.

In the reaction.

In the choice to stay steady without becoming cruel. Boundaries that build trust are not performances of strength. Professionally, this matters because boundary language protects roles, scope, ethical functioning, and professional integrity. A clinician without boundaries can drift into overfunctioning. A supervisor without boundaries can rescue instead of develop. A leader without boundaries can create confusion and call it flexibility. A helper without boundaries can eventually become resentful toward the very people they are trying to serve. Boundaries protect the person, the relationship, and the work. They are practices of responsibility.

They teach you that your limits can exist without apology.

They teach others where you stand. They give relationships a chance to become honest. They give confidence the evidence it needs.

I can be clear.

I can survive discomfort.

I can tolerate someone's reaction.

I can repair without erasing myself.

I can stay kind and still have a spine.

Practice Point

Notice This

Where do you avoid boundaries because you do not want to tolerate the reaction? Look for places where you over-explain, say yes when you mean no, or stay silent to preserve comfort.

Try This

Set one small, clear boundary this week. Make it behavioral, specific, and connected to what you will do. Do not over-explain it. Practice holding it.

Measure This

Track your follow-through, not the other person's response. Did you maintain the boundary when discomfort showed up? Confidence grows when clarity and action match.

Chapter 10: Accountability Without Shame

Accountability has a branding problem. The word walks into the room and everyone immediately starts looking for an exit.

It has the energy of a calendar invite titled "quick chat" from someone who uses no punctuation.

It arrives with all the charm of an unread email from a supervisor that says, "quick question."

Some people hear the word and immediately brace for punishment.

They think of blame.

Humiliation.

Harshness.

Being called out.

Being exposed.

Being told they are bad.

Being cornered by someone who claims to value growth but seems a little too excited to deliver a verbal performance review of their entire personality.

So accountability gets avoided.

Softened.

Reframed.

Delayed.

Turned into something more comfortable.

People say, “I do not want to shame myself.”

That can be wise. Shame is not a good teacher when it becomes identity.

Shame says, “I am bad.”

Guilt, when it is proportionate and connected to behavior, can be useful.

Accountability in actual life

In relationships, accountability may sound like, “I got defensive and shifted the focus away from what you were trying to tell me.” In work, it may sound like, “I missed the deadline, and I need to communicate earlier next time.” In therapy, it may sound like, “I understand why avoidance makes sense, and I still need to practice the exposure.” In supervision, it may sound like, “I was unsure and waited too long to ask for support.” In personal growth, it may sound like, "I keep saying I want confidence, but I am not giving myself evidence."

None of those sentences require self-hatred.

They require ownership.

That is why shame is such a poor substitute for accountability. Shame keeps the focus on identity. Accountability keeps the focus on responsibility and repair. Shame says, "What does this mean about me?" Accountability asks, "What needs to happen next?"

That next question is where movement begins.

Guilt says, "I did something misaligned."

Shame says, "I am bad."

Accountability says, "I can own what happened, repair where needed, and practice differently." Shame and guilt do different things to responsibility and repair, yet they often get collapsed together (Tangney & Dearing, 2002). Once that happens, people either avoid responsibility because they fear shame, or drown in shame and never move into responsibility.

Accountability says, "Something needs to be owned."

Those are different.

Shame collapses the self.

Accountability strengthens the self.

Shame often leads to hiding, defensiveness, over-explaining, attacking, or giving up. Accountability creates the possibility of repair, growth, responsibility, and change. A culture that confuses accountability with shame will avoid one of the most important tools for confidence. Confidence does not grow only from being praised. Confidence grows from knowing you can face yourself honestly and remain intact.

That is emotional adulthood.

Not perfection.

Not never messing up.

Not never hurting someone.

Not never avoiding, reacting, forgetting, missing the mark, saying it poorly, becoming defensive, or making a decision that future you reviews with a facial expression. Emotional adulthood is the ability to tell the truth about your impact, repair where needed, learn from the pattern, and stay responsible without turning the entire moment into self-hatred.

Accountability without shame sounds like:

"I did that."

"That was not okay."

"I can understand why I reacted that way, and I am still responsible for what I did."

"I need to repair this."

"I avoided it."

"I was defensive."

"I crossed a line."

"I did not follow through."

"I let fear make that decision."

"I need to practice differently."

Notice what is missing.

There is no self-destruction.

No identity collapse.

No dramatic speech about being the worst person alive. No using guilt to avoid change. No making the harmed person comfort you because accountability feels uncomfortable.

That performance may feel honest, but it often makes the injured person audition for the role of comforter.

Accountability does not require self-abandonment.

It requires ownership.

Some of the feedback that strengthened me did not feel delightful when it arrived and that's alright because growth rarely knocks politely with a fruit basket. There have been moments in supervision, leadership, writing, and relationships where I had to sit with the uncomfortable reality that my intention did not erase my impact. I did not need to hate myself but I did need to listen, own what was mine, and practice differently.

I have wanted accountability to arrive softer. Preferably wrapped in reassurance, carrying snacks, and making it very clear that I am still lovable before asking me to change. Sometimes love does that. Sometimes love also tells the truth and expects me to stay in the room.

This matters because many people use shame to avoid accountability while appearing remorseful.

They move quickly into, "I am terrible."

"I ruin everything."

"I cannot do anything right."

"I guess I am just a bad person."

"I hate myself."

At first, this may look like accountability.

It is not. It often shifts attention away from the impact and back onto the person's distress. Now the conversation becomes about reassuring them.

Now the repair gets delayed. Now the person who was hurt may feel responsible for making the other person feel better. Shame can become another form of avoidance.

Not always intentionally.

Functionally.

The question is not, "Do I feel bad enough?"

Feeling terrible is not a repair plan. It is just a very exhausting weather system.

Feeling bad enough is not the goal.

Repair has to become behavioral

Repair is not proved by intensity. It is not proved by crying, over-explaining, apologizing repeatedly, or making sure everyone knows how awful you feel. Those things may happen, but they are not the repair.

Repair becomes real when behavior changes.

That may mean naming the impact specifically. It may mean making amends. It may mean changing the pattern that caused the harm. It may mean accepting that trust may take time to rebuild. It may mean tolerating the discomfort of not being immediately reassured.

A mature apology does not demand that the other person resolve your shame. It offers ownership and then practices change.

This is why accountability without shame builds confidence. It teaches you that you can face something true about your behavior without collapsing into worthlessness. You can be imperfect and still responsible. You can be ashamed and still repair. You can regret something and still move forward differently.

That is not small. That is emotional strength.

Repair is the goal.

Changed behavior is the goal.

Clear ownership is the goal.

A person can feel terrible and still not repair anything. A person can feel ashamed and still avoid responsibility. A person can give a dramatic apology and still repeat the pattern. Accountability asks for movement, not performance.

The question is, "Am I willing to be responsible?" Responsibility is more useful than self-punishment. In therapy, that matters enormously. A client may need validation for why a pattern developed, but that does not mean the pattern has no impact. A person may have trauma, anxiety, depression, diagnosed ADHD, learning differences, executive-function challenges, grief, attachment wounds, or a history that explains why certain responses make sense.

Explanation matters.

It helps reduce shame.

It creates context.

It guides support.

Explanation is not exemption from responsibility. This is where compassion needs a spine.

Compassion says, “There is a reason this is hard.”

The spine says, “And you are still responsible for how you respond.”

Both are necessary.

Without compassion, accountability becomes punishment.

Without accountability, compassion becomes enabling.

A person can have a reason and still need to repair. A person can be struggling and still need to follow through. A person can be triggered and still need to avoid causing harm. A person can be overwhelmed and still need to communicate. A person can be hurt and still need to take responsibility for how they treat others.

This is not harsh.

It is relationally necessary.

Relationships cannot survive on validation alone.

They require repair.

They require honesty.

They require ownership.

They require the ability to say, “My pain is real, and so is my impact.” That sentence keeps two truths in the room at the same time.

It refuses to erase the pain. It also refuses to erase the impact. It prevents a person from using suffering as a shield against responsibility. It also prevents accountability from becoming a weapon that ignores context. This is the kind of dialectic emotional adulthood requires. That sentence is powerful. It keeps people from using their wounds as weapons. It also keeps people from using accountability as cruelty. Both matter. Accountability builds confidence because it teaches you that mistakes are survivable.

Avoiding accountability makes mistakes feel catastrophic. If you cannot face a mistake, every mistake becomes a threat to your identity. If you can face a mistake, it becomes information.

Painful information, perhaps.

Important information, definitely.

Information you can use.

This is how competence develops.

At work, accountability helps people grow. Feedback may be uncomfortable, but without it, performance cannot improve. A person who interprets all correction as personal attack will struggle to build skill because every learning moment becomes a threat. In relationships, accountability helps people repair. A person who cannot own impact will keep repeating patterns and calling themselves misunderstood. In personal growth, accountability helps people stop outsourcing responsibility. A person who blames every limitation on circumstances may feel temporarily protected, but they also lose access to agency.

Agency is central to confidence.

Not control over everything.

Agency.

The ability to ask, "What belongs to me here?"

Not everything belongs to you.

Other people's behavior does not belong to you.

Systems may create real barriers.

Trauma may create real wounds.

Mental-health symptoms may create real impairment.

Family patterns may shape real responses.

Culture may reinforce real distortions.

None of that should be minimized.

If nothing belongs to you, then nothing can be practiced. If nothing can be practiced, confidence has nowhere to grow.

Accountability returns a person to agency.

It says, "This part is mine."

"My response is mine."

"My repair is mine."

"My follow-through is mine."

"My avoidance is mine."

"My next repetition is mine."

"My willingness is mine."

That is not blame.

That is power.

A lot of people fear accountability because they think it will make them feel small.

Healthy accountability does the opposite.

It makes you more solid.

It teaches you that you can tell the truth and survive it.

You can own impact without becoming worthless.

You can receive feedback without disappearing.

You can repair without groveling.

You can change without hating who you were before.

You can be responsible without carrying what is not yours.

That is confidence with a spine.

Not confidence that depends on always being right. Confidence that can stay present when you are not. This is the kind of confidence that changes relationships, workplaces, therapy, supervision, parenting, leadership, and the private life you have with yourself.

It is not flashy.

It is not always comfortable.

It is deeply sturdy.

Accountability without shame is not, "You are bad."

It is, “You are capable of owning this.”

It is not, “You should have known better, so suffer.”

It is, “Now that you know, practice differently.”

It is not, “Your reasons do not matter.”

It is, “Your reasons matter, and your impact still matters, too.”

It is not, “Be perfect.”

It is, “Be honest. Repair. Learn. Repeat.”

That is the work.

Not self-punishment.

Not avoidance.

Practice.

Practice Point

Notice This

Where do you collapse into shame instead of practicing accountability? Look for moments where “I am terrible” replaces “I need to own this.”

Try This

Choose one small area where responsibility belongs to you. Name it plainly without attacking yourself. Then identify one repair or next action.

Measure This

Did accountability lead to movement? Did you repair, follow through, clarify, apologize, adjust, or practice differently? Confidence grows when you can face yourself without abandoning yourself.

Part II names what actually builds confidence: evidence, discomfort tolerance, self-regulation, boundaries, and accountability.

Confidence is not a mood.

It is not a performance.

It is not something you wait for until life feels easy. Confidence grows when compassion has enough structure to help you practice. Part III will move deeper into the framework underneath all of this:

Compassion with a Spine.

PART III

Compassion with a Spine

Compassion is one of the most necessary forces in healing. It is also one of the most misunderstood. In some spaces, compassion has been reduced to softness.

Agreement.

Comfort.

Protection from distress.

A refusal to challenge anything that may activate shame, fear, defensiveness, or discomfort. In other spaces, compassion is dismissed as weakness: something too soft for accountability, too emotional for standards, too gentle for reality, too permissive for growth.

Both misunderstand it. One turns compassion into a pillow. The other turns the spine into a hammer. Neither helps anyone build a life.

A pillow cannot hold a standard. A hammer cannot hold a person.

Compassion is not the absence of structure.

It is not the absence of truth.

It is not the absence of expectation.

It is not the removal of discomfort.

Compassion is the willingness to remain connected to a person's humanity while still telling the truth about what growth requires. That kind of compassion needs a spine. Without a spine, compassion collapses into accommodation.

Without compassion, the spine becomes severity.

This section names the framework underneath the entire book.

This phrase did not emerge as branding first.

It emerged from observation: from clinical rooms where validation helped but avoidance still organized the client's life, from supervision spaces where kindness without standards left developing clinicians underprepared, from workplaces where discomfort was avoided until problems became patterns, and from my own life, where softness alone was not enough and hardness alone was not healing.

Compassion with a Spine became the language for what actually seemed to help: warmth that did not collapse, truth that did not injure, support that did not enable, and standards that did not lose their humanity. Eventually, I realized I was not just naming a professional concern. I was naming my philosophy of healing; how I have treated myself in my own growth, and how the best supports around me called out my nonsense instead of gliding over it.

That kind of support is not always fun in the moment. It is deeply inconvenient to be loved by people who can see the difference between your wound and your excuse. It is also one of the reasons I trust this framework.

Compassion with a Spine rests on five pillars:

Capability over fragility.

Boundaries as care.

Accountability as compassion.

Functioning as the metric of progress.

Emotional adulthood as the goal.

These pillars apply clinically, relationally, professionally, personally, and culturally. They belong in therapy rooms, supervision spaces, classrooms, workplaces, families, leadership, friendships, and the private conversation a person has with themselves when fear is loud and avoidance looks tempting.

They are not slogans.

They are standards.

They are the structure that allows compassion to strengthen instead of soothe people into staying stuck. Part I named what has been shrinking. Part II named what actually builds confidence. Part III names the framework that holds it together.

Chapter 11: The Five Pillars of Compassion with a Spine

A framework matters because language needs structure. Without structure, even good language can drift. Language without structure is like a room without walls: everything important is technically there, but nothing has enough shape to hold.

Why this framework had to be named

I did not need another phrase. I needed a structure for what I kept seeing. The same problem was appearing in different rooms with different language: care without expectation, validation without direction, boundaries without responsibility, support without movement, standards without enough warmth, warmth without enough structure.

In therapy, the pattern could look like endless understanding without functional change. In supervision, it could look like protecting a developing clinician from discomfort instead of helping them grow through it. In leadership, it could look like avoiding hard conversations until inconsistency became culture. In personal life, it could look like calling every avoided step peace because honesty felt too exposing.

The phrase compassion with a spine gave shape to the correction.

It did not ask me to choose between care and truth. It insisted that the work needed both. That is why the framework belongs here. It gives the book a structure that can hold the GWC softness and the PIP standard without letting either one distort the other.

Compassion becomes comfort.

Boundaries become control.

Accountability becomes shame.

Validation becomes agreement.

Safety becomes avoidance.

Confidence becomes performance.

Healing becomes whatever feels relieving in the moment.

This is how drift happens.

Not with a villain cape. Usually with a very reasonable tone and a sentence that starts with, "I just do not want to make it worse."

Rarely all at once.

Rarely with bad intentions.

Usually through small shifts that seem caring, reasonable, or protective in isolation, but begin to weaken the work when they become the pattern. I have watched this happen through good people with good intentions. That is part of why it matters so much. Most drift does not begin with someone deciding to abandon standards. It takes shape with someone not wanting to hurt, disappoint, overwhelm, or be misunderstood. I understand that impulse; I've lived both sides of that impulse. I have felt the pull to soften something true because I did not want the discomfort that might follow. I also know how quickly care can lose its shape when discomfort becomes the thing everyone organizes around. A clinician avoids challenging a client because the client becomes tearful. A parent lowers every expectation because a child feels overwhelmed. A supervisor softens every piece of feedback because a new clinician feels anxious. A partner stops bringing up concerns because conflict feels too activating. A person abandons a goal because insecurity rises. A workplace avoids accountability because morale is fragile. In each moment, the intention may be compassion. Intention is not the same as impact.

Compassion has to be measured by what it produces.

This is where the work gets less cute and more honest.

Does it build capacity?

Does it clarify responsibility?

Does it strengthen functioning?

Does it preserve dignity without avoiding truth? Does it help the person become more capable of meeting life? Or does it simply reduce discomfort in the moment?

That question is the spine. Compassion with a Spine is not a rejection of warmth.

It is the part that keeps compassion from becoming a very nice-looking exit ramp.

It is warmth with structure.

It is not a rejection of validation.

It is validation with direction.

It is not a rejection of support.

It is support that strengthens.

It is not a rejection of softness.

It is softness that does not collapse when discomfort enters the room. The five pillars give the framework shape. The pillars came from watching what held up over time. In clinical work, I noticed that people did not only need to feel understood. They needed to become more able. In supervision, I noticed that developing professionals did not only need reassurance. They needed structure, feedback, and room to practice judgment. In relationships and daily life, I noticed the same thing: the patterns that created immediate relief often weakened long-term confidence. The framework formed around what corrected that drift.

How the pillars correct drift

Each pillar corrects a specific form of drift.

Capability over fragility corrects the drift toward overprotection. It protects the belief that people can be supported without being reduced to incapability.

Boundaries as care corrects the drift toward blurry compassion. It protects roles, limits, trust, and the work from becoming dependent on overextension.

Accountability as compassion corrects the drift toward avoiding responsibility in the name of kindness. It protects agency, repair, and the dignity of being treated as capable of ownership.

Functioning as the metric of progress corrects the drift toward insight without movement. It protects the connection between healing and lived life.

Emotional adulthood as the goal corrects the drift toward letting feelings become the final authority. It protects responsibility without demanding emotional numbness.

Together, the pillars keep compassion from dissolving into something vague. They give care a shape. They give growth a direction. They give confidence something to stand on.

They protect compassion from becoming vague.

They protect accountability from becoming harsh.

They protect confidence from becoming performative.

They protect healing from becoming avoidance.

The first pillar is capability over fragility.

It corrects the overprotection of discomfort.

It protects the person's growth potential.

When it is missing, support can become a quiet agreement that the person is too delicate to practice. This means we do not build people around the belief that they are too delicate to tolerate life. We honor pain, symptoms, history, and limitation without making fragility the organizing principle of the person's identity.

Capability asks, "What can be strengthened here?"

It does not ask, "How do we make sure this person never feels activated?" The second pillar is boundaries as care. It corrects the belief that love, therapy, leadership, or service require unlimited access. It protects clarity, roles, limits, and trust. When it is missing, resentment and overfunctioning begin to look like devotion.

Boundaries are not punishment.

They are not rejection.

They are not control dressed up in clinical language. Boundaries are the structure that allows people, relationships, systems, and work to remain honest.

They clarify what belongs to whom.

They reduce resentment.

They make trust possible because they connect words to action. The third pillar is accountability as compassion. It corrects the confusion between responsibility and shame. It protects repair, agency, and ethical growth. When it is missing, compassion becomes enabling and the pattern remains untouched.

Accountability is not shame.

It is not cruelty.

It is not a performance of moral superiority.

Accountability is the belief that a person is capable of ownership, repair, and change. To remove accountability from someone's life is not compassion. It is a quiet statement that you do not believe they can handle responsibility. The fourth pillar is functioning as the metric of progress. It corrects the overreliance on insight as proof of change. It protects the connection between healing and lived life. When it is missing, a person may understand everything and still become less able to live.

Feelings matter.

Insight matters.

Validation matters.

If functioning keeps declining while language keeps expanding, something is incomplete. Progress cannot be measured only by how understood a person feels. It has to include what the person is becoming able to do.

Can they engage?

Can they tolerate?

Can they repair?

Can they follow through?

Can they preserve responsibilities?

Can they move toward values even when discomfort is present? The fifth pillar's goal is emotional adulthood. It corrects the idea that feelings should either be obeyed or suppressed. It protects responsibility in the presence of emotion. When it is missing, emotional intensity begins deciding what truth, accountability, and connection are allowed to survive.

Emotional adulthood is not emotional suppression.

It is not becoming unbothered.

It is not never needing help.

It is the practiced ability to feel deeply while remaining responsible for your behavior. It means you can experience anxiety without making avoidance your life plan.

You can feel shame without collapsing into self-hatred.

You can feel anger without becoming destructive.

You can feel guilt without abandoning your boundaries.

You can feel hurt without using pain as permission to harm.

These five pillars work together.

Capability gives the person a growth direction.

Boundaries provide structure.

Accountability returns agency.

Functioning measures whether growth is translating into life. Emotional adulthood keeps feeling connected to responsibility.

This framework is not harsh.

It is sturdy.

It does not ask people to stop being human. It asks them to stop treating humanness as evidence of helplessness. It does not shame people for struggling. It asks whether the struggle is being met with practices that build capacity. It does not tell clinicians, parents, leaders, partners, or individuals to become harder.

It asks them to become steadier.

There is a difference.

Hardness loses access to compassion.

Steadiness keeps compassion connected to truth.

That is the heart of this framework. Compassion with a Spine is not about becoming less caring. It is about caring enough to stop confusing comfort with growth.

Practice Point

Notice This

Where has compassion become vague in your life or work? Look for places where support is present, but structure, accountability, or growth is missing.

Try This

Choose one situation and ask: "What would compassion with a spine require here?" Identify both parts: the compassion and the spine. For example, the compassion may be naming the fear honestly; the spine may be choosing one supported next step instead of letting the fear run the whole plan.

Measure This

Did the response build capacity, clarify responsibility, or strengthen functioning? If it only reduced discomfort, something may still be missing.

Chapter 12: Capability Over Fragility

Capability comes first because every other part of the framework depends on it.

It is the load-bearing wall of this whole house.

Boundaries require capability.

Accountability requires capability.

Functioning requires capability.

Emotional adulthood requires capability.

Confidence requires capability.

Without capability, every difficult feeling becomes a threat.

Every hard conversation becomes too much.

Every boundary becomes a rupture.

Every piece of feedback becomes a personal attack.

Every responsibility becomes overwhelming.

Every growth opportunity becomes evidence of insufficiency.

The person may have language.

They may have insight.

They may have support.

They may have validation.

Without capability, life remains organized around what they believe they cannot tolerate.

That is fragility.

Not because the person is weak, but because the pattern has been rehearsed until shrinking starts to feel like wisdom.

Again, fragility is not sensitivity.

It is not trauma.

It is not depression.

It is not anxiety.

It is not grief.

It is not needing support.

It is not being emotional, tender, reactive, overwhelmed, or in pain. Fragility is the repeated pattern of organizing life around the assumption of incapability.

It says:

"I cannot handle this."

"I should not have to feel this."

"If it is uncomfortable, something is wrong."

"If I am activated, I should stop."

"If accountability hurts, it must be harmful."

"If a relationship has tension, it must be unsafe."

"If I feel anxious, I am not ready."

"If I struggle, I am failing."

Fragility turns discomfort into evidence.

Evidence of danger.

Evidence of limitation.

Evidence that the demand should be lowered. Evidence that the world must adjust before the person can practice.

Capability tells a different story.

Capability says:

"This is hard, and I can learn."

"This is uncomfortable, and I can stay present."

"This is activating, and I can slow down without disappearing."

"This is new, and I can practice."

"This is feedback, and I can use what is useful."

"This is tension, and I can remain honest."

"This is fear, and it does not get to make every decision."

Capability does not deny difficulty.

It gives difficulty somewhere to go.

A capable person still feels anxiety.

They still feel sadness.

They still feel shame.

They still feel fear.

They still need help, rest, guidance, treatment, support, and repair. The difference is that these experiences do not automatically become the boundary of their life. Capability is not something people either have or do not have. I have had to remind myself of this more than once. Capability rarely announces itself before the first repetition. It certainly does not walk in with a clipboard and say, "Congratulations, you are now ready." More often, capability shows up after you have done the hard thing enough times that your body finally starts believing you might survive it.

I have seen that in my professional life, my writing, my leadership, my confidence, my body, my relationships, and the private places where fear tries to sound wise. I did not become capable because I waited until everything felt easy. I became more capable because I kept practicing the next honest thing with support, structure, and a moderately dramatic amount of internal commentary.

I would love to tell you capability felt noble while it was forming. More often, it felt awkward, exposed, and deeply unphotogenic. Growth does not always look inspiring while it is happening. Sometimes it looks like doing the thing anyway while your brain files a formal complaint.

My internal commentary, for the record, is rarely concise.

Capability is not independence without support.

Supported does not mean carried.

Support should not become a substitute for capability. It should become the structure that helps capability develop.

A supported person is not abandoned to figure everything out alone. They are also not carried so completely that they never discover what they can hold. The difference matters.

In parenting, support may mean staying near while a child practices frustration, rather than removing every frustration immediately. In supervision, support may mean helping a new clinician think through a case, rather than handing them every answer before judgment can develop. In therapy, support may mean pacing exposure carefully, rather than avoiding exposure because anxiety rises. In adult life, support may mean asking for help with the first step, not outsourcing the entire task.

Being supported should not shrink a person's world. Done well, support gives them enough steadiness to re-enter it.

That is the dignity of capability. It says, "You do not have to do this alone, and you are still part of the doing."

It is supported growth in capacity. It means a person is given enough structure to practice, enough support to remain engaged, and enough expectation to keep growing. A person may need accommodation and still be capable. A person may need treatment and still be capable. A person may need rest and still be capable. Capability is not the absence of need. It is the presence of practiced ability.

It is built.

Through repetition.

Through exposure.

Through support.

Through follow-through.

Through small acts of doing what fear said was impossible. Through tolerating discomfort long enough to collect new evidence. This is why treating someone as capable is not the same as abandoning them. There is a shallow version of capability that sounds like, "Figure it out." That is not this framework. There is a harsh version that sounds like, "Other people have it worse, so stop complaining." That is not this framework. There is a dismissive version that sounds like, "You are fine. Just do it."

That is not a framework; that is a bumper sticker with abandonment issues.

That is not this framework.

Compassion with a Spine says:

"I believe this is hard."

"I believe your pain is real."

"I believe your history matters."

"I believe support may be necessary."

"And I also believe you are capable of building more capacity than fear is currently allowing you to see."

That is different.

That is not dismissal.

That is dignity.

To treat a person as capable is to respect their potential for growth. It is to refuse to reduce them to symptoms, history, diagnosis, fear, or current functioning. It is to see both the wound and the person beyond the wound. In clinical work, this matters deeply. A client who has avoided driving because of panic may feel genuinely terrified behind the wheel.

Compassion validates the fear. The spine builds a plan for exposure. A client with depression may feel no motivation to complete basic tasks.

Compassion validates the heaviness. The spine identifies one small behavioral step. A client who avoids conflict may feel overwhelmed by boundaries.

Compassion validates the relational fear. The spine helps them practice direct communication. A client who becomes defensive during feedback may feel shame quickly.

Compassion validates the shame.

The spine returns to accountability.

In each case, the goal is not to overwhelm the person.

The goal is to strengthen them.

This applies outside therapy, too.

A parent treating a child as capable does not ignore distress. They help the child practice tolerating frustration, problem-solving, apologizing, trying again, waiting, asking for help, and experiencing disappointment without collapsing. A supervisor treating a clinician as capable does not shame uncertainty. They provide structure, feedback, modeling, and opportunities to practice clinical judgment. A partner treating a loved one as capable does not dismiss emotions. They allow emotions to exist without making them the only authority in the relationship. A person treating themselves as capable does not bully themselves into productivity; they stop assuming discomfort means they are unable.

That shift matters. A person who believes they are fragile will often seek less life.

Less challenge.

Less risk.

Less feedback.

Less exposure.

Less honesty.

Less responsibility.

Less growth.

A person practicing capability begins to seek more capacity.

Not more overwhelm.

More capacity.

There is a difference.

Capacity grows best at the edge of what is tolerable, not in the center of what is comfortable and not in the chaos of what is overwhelming. This is the growth edge. Not the center of comfort, where nothing new is asked. Not the chaos of overwhelm, where the person cannot integrate what is happening. The growth edge is the place where the task is challenging enough to require practice and supported enough to remain possible. A child learning frustration tolerance needs that edge. A new clinician learning feedback tolerance needs that edge. A client practicing exposure needs that edge. An adult rebuilding confidence after avoidance needs that edge.

The edge is personal

The growth edge is not the same size for every person. For one person, the edge may be speaking in a meeting. For another, it may be leaving the house. For another, it may be receiving feedback without shutting down. For another, it may be resting without calling rest laziness. For another, it may be admitting they need help.

This is why compassion with a spine cannot be one-size-fits-all.

The spine asks for movement. Compassion helps determine the size and timing of the movement.

Too much challenge can flood a person into shutdown. Too little challenge can teach a person that they are incapable of more. The art is in finding the next honest step: small enough to be possible, meaningful enough to matter.

That step is where capability grows.

Too much demand can flood the system. Too little demand can keep the system underdeveloped. The edge is where capability is built. That edge is where compassion and spine work together.

Compassion prevents recklessness.

The spine prevents retreat.

Compassion asks, "What support is needed?" The spine asks, "What practice is required?" Compassion asks, "What is the wound?" The spine asks, "What is the next step?" Compassion asks, "What needs protection?" The spine asks, "What needs strengthening?" Capability grows when both questions are allowed in the room. This is also where confidence grows. Confidence does not come from being told endlessly that you are capable. It comes from experiencing yourself doing capable things.

Small things count.

Sending the email.

Opening the bill.

Making the appointment.

Setting the boundary.

Repairing the conflict.

Taking the walk.

Trying the class.

Asking for feedback.

Returning after avoidance.

Completing the task while anxious.

Following through when motivation is absent.

Every repetition says, "I am becoming someone who can."

Not loudly. More like a stubborn little sticky note your nervous system eventually has to respect.

That is capability.

Not perfection.

Not constant strength.

Not endless resilience without rest.

A practiced relationship with difficulty.

You do not need the world to shrink for you to survive it. You need the capacity to expand within it.

That capacity can be built.

It begins with refusing to make fragility your identity.

Practice Point

Notice This

Where do you assume incapability before you have practiced capacity? Look for places where "I cannot" may actually mean "I have not built this yet."

Try This

Choose one area where you have been treating yourself as fragile. Identify one small supported practice that would build capability without overwhelming you.

Measure This

Did the practice expand your behavioral range? Capability grows when your life becomes slightly larger, not when discomfort disappears.

Chapter 13: Boundaries as Care

Boundaries are often treated as defensive.

A way to protect yourself.

A way to keep people out.

A way to stop being used, drained, overwhelmed, manipulated, or pulled into what does not belong to you.

That is part of it.

It is not the whole thing.

Boundaries are also care. They care for the person setting them. They care for the relationship by making honesty possible. They care for the work by protecting roles, responsibilities, and standards. They care for the system by clarifying what belongs where. They care for trust because they make follow-through visible.

Without boundaries, compassion becomes blurry. A person says yes while building resentment. A clinician overfunctions and calls it care.

A supervisor rescues instead of teaching. A leader avoids correction to preserve morale. A family member absorbs responsibility that belongs to someone else. A friend becomes endlessly available and then quietly bitter. A partner avoids honesty and calls it peace. The absence of boundaries often looks generous at first.

Over time, it becomes expensive.

The bill usually comes later, with interest, resentment, and one deeply tired nervous system.

Resentment always sends an invoice.

The cost is resentment.

Confusion.

Over-functioning.

Dependency.

Avoidance.

Dishonesty.

Emotional exhaustion.

A relationship or system without boundaries may look close, but closeness without clarity is unstable. People do not always know where they stand.

Expectations become assumed instead of communicated. Limits are discovered only after someone exceeds them. Conflict becomes harder because no one has practiced naming what is true.

Boundaries prevent that drift.

They make the invisible visible.

They say:

"This is my limit."

"This is my role."

"This is your responsibility."

"This is what I can offer."

"This is what I cannot continue."

"This is what will happen if the pattern does not change."

That clarity is not cruelty.

It is care.

The challenge is that boundaries often create discomfort.

People may feel disappointed.

They may feel surprised.

They may feel angry.

They may misunderstand.

They may push back.

They may accuse the boundary-setter of being selfish, harsh, distant, rigid, dramatic, cold, or different than they used to be.

Sometimes that last one is true.

Growth does make people different.

A person who begins setting boundaries will be different from the version of themselves who stayed silent, overgave, overexplained, overfunctioned, or absorbed everything to keep the peace. That difference can unsettle the people who benefited from the old pattern. This is why boundaries require capacity. Without distress tolerance, a person may set a boundary and then immediately abandon it when discomfort rises.

They may soften it.

Explain it repeatedly.

Apologize for it unnecessarily.

Turn it into a maybe.

Make exceptions that recreate the original problem. Take responsibility for the other person's reaction. Call the boundary wrong because it did not feel good. Boundaries are not proven wrong by discomfort. Sometimes discomfort is evidence that the boundary is touching an old pattern. If you were taught to be agreeable, a boundary may feel rude. If you were taught to manage everyone's emotions, a boundary may feel selfish. If you were taught love requires self-abandonment, a boundary may feel like rejection. If you were taught conflict is dangerous, a boundary may feel unsafe.

The feeling is real.

It may not be accurate.

This is where compassion with a spine becomes essential. Compassion says, "Of course this feels hard. There is history here." The spine says, "The discomfort does not automatically mean you should abandon the boundary."

Both are needed.

Boundaries also require responsibility.

A boundary is not a speech.

It is not a threat.

It is not an attempt to control someone else's entire personality. It is not a demand that everyone behave exactly as you prefer so that you never have to feel activated. A boundary is a statement of what you will do in response to what is happening.

It is connected to your behavior.

That is what gives it integrity.

"I need you to stop being disrespectful" may be a request. "If yelling continues, I am going to pause this conversation and come back later" is a boundary.

"You cannot text me like that" may be a demand.

"I am not going to respond to insulting messages" is a boundary.

"You need to respect my time" may be a value. "I need twenty-four hours' notice before committing to plans" is a boundary. Boundaries become clearer when they are behavioral.

What will you do?

What will you not do?

What will you participate in?

What will you leave?

What will you continue?

What will you stop rescuing, absorbing, explaining, or carrying? Boundaries as care also matter clinically and professionally. A therapist who does not hold boundaries may become overavailable, inconsistent, rescuing, or unclear. That does not help the client build capacity. It may create dependency or confusion. A supervisor who does not hold boundaries may avoid necessary feedback. That does not protect the supervisee. It delays growth and may compromise the work. A workplace that does not hold boundaries around standards may call itself supportive while allowing drift, resentment, and inconsistency to spread. A helping professional without boundaries may confuse compassion with overextension until burnout arrives with a clipboard and a list of ignored warning signs.

Burnout is not subtle when it finally gets tired of being ignored.

Boundaries protect the work. Boundaries protect the work from becoming dependent on individual overfunctioning. They prevent care from relying on one person's endless availability, emotional labor, or willingness to absorb what a system has not clarified. They protect clinician availability, scope of practice, supervision roles, workplace expectations, documentation standards, and the basic truth that helping work still needs structure.

Over-functioning is not the same as care

Over-functioning can feel noble because it is often wrapped in responsibility. The person who overfunctions may look dedicated, reliable, compassionate, and endlessly useful. They answer faster. They stay later. They absorb more. They rescue what systems fail to structure. They become the person everyone can count on because they keep proving they will carry what no one else has clarified.

At first, this may protect the work.

Over time, it distorts it.

The work begins depending on individual self-abandonment instead of clear roles, adequate systems, and shared responsibility. Resentment grows. Burnout becomes predictable. Standards become person-dependent rather than structure-dependent.

Boundaries interrupt that pattern.

They say care cannot be built on endless absorption. They say helping work still needs limits.

They say compassion is not measured by how much of yourself you erase.

That is why boundaries are not a side issue in professional integrity. They are part of what keeps the work honest.

They protect the field.

They protect the people we serve.

I have had to learn that overfunctioning is not the same as caring more. In helping work especially, it is easy to confuse exhaustion with commitment and availability with compassion. The problem is that a person cannot protect the work by disappearing into it. At some point, the boundary is not what makes the work less compassionate. It is what keeps compassion from becoming unsustainable. They also protect the person doing the work from becoming absorbed by it. This is why boundaries are not the opposite of compassion. They are one of compassion's structures.

I know the seduction of being useful. Usefulness can feel like safety, belonging, excellence, and love all rolled into one very tired person. If being needed becomes the only proof that you matter, boundaries will feel like betrayal even when they are actually rescue.

A boundary says, “This matters enough to be clear.”

Clarity is care with its shoes on.

“This relationship matters enough to be honest.”

“This work matters enough to protect.”

“This person matters enough not to enable.”

“I matter enough not to disappear.”

That is care.

Not the sentimental kind.

The sturdy kind.

The kind that can tolerate being misunderstood for a moment because clarity matters more than performance. The kind that knows trust is not built by saying yes to everything. The kind that understands that resentment is not proof of love. The kind that refuses to confuse availability with devotion.

Boundaries are where confidence becomes visible.

Not loud confidence.

Not harsh confidence.

Not the performative kind that announces itself in captions and then collapses the moment someone is disappointed.

Steady confidence.

The kind that says:

"I can be kind and clear."

"I can be loving and limited."

"I can be generous and honest."

"I can be responsible without carrying what is not mine."

"I can tolerate the discomfort of being misunderstood."

"I can hold the line without becoming cruel."

That kind of confidence is built through practice.

One clear sentence.

One honest limit.

One follow-through.

One moment of not apologizing for having a boundary that needed to exist. Boundaries as care do not make life free of discomfort.

They make life more honest.

Honest is where growth can actually begin.

Practice Point

Notice This

Where are boundaries missing, unclear, or inconsistently held? Look for resentment, overextension, repeated confusion, and places where you keep hoping someone will notice a limit you have not clearly named.

Try This

Write one boundary in behavioral terms. Use this structure: "If this happens, I will do this." Keep it clear, kind, and specific.

Measure This

Did the boundary create clarity? Did you follow through? Boundaries build confidence when they move from intention to action.

Chapter 14: Accountability as Compassion

Accountability is one of the clearest places where compassion has lost its spine. The word itself can make people defensive.

Accountability sounds like blame.

Correction.

Punishment.

Being exposed.

Being shamed.

Being told to take responsibility by someone who seems a little too energized by the opportunity.

So people avoid it.

They soften the language.

They overvalidate the feeling.

They focus on intent instead of impact. They explain the reason so thoroughly that responsibility disappears. They avoid the conversation because discomfort might rise.

This is often framed as compassion. Accountability is not the enemy of compassion. Accountability is one of its strongest expressions. To hold someone accountable is to believe they are capable of ownership.

Capable of repair.

Capable of change.

Capable of facing the truth without being destroyed by it.

That is not cruelty.

That is respect.

The opposite of accountability is not kindness. The opposite of accountability is often a quiet form of disbelief. Some of the people who helped me grow the most were not the ones who only reassured me. They were the ones who believed I could handle truth. Not cruelty. Not unnecessary sharpness. Truth. There is a particular kind of respect in being held to a standard by someone who still sees your humanity.

I say that carefully because I have benefited from people believing I could handle more truth than I wanted in the moment. Not because they were cruel. They respected me enough not to make my comfort the highest goal.

It says, "I do not think you can handle this."

"I do not think you can own your impact."

"I do not think you can repair."

"I do not think you can tolerate the discomfort of responsibility."

"I do not think you can grow."

That may feel gentle in the moment.

It is not empowering. Accountability as compassion refuses to treat people as too fragile for truth. It also refuses to use truth as a weapon.

Both matter.

Some people use accountability harshly.

They confuse directness with dominance.

They correct without care.

They shame and call it standards.

They humiliate and call it honesty.

They punish and call it growth.

That is not accountability with compassion.

That is severity wearing a professional outfit.

The outfit is usually crisp. The impact is still ugly.

It may have a blazer, but it is still harm.

Healthy accountability has structure.

Accountability and punishment are not the same thing.

Accountability in systems

Systems also need accountability because systems can drift while everyone inside them insists they are trying their best. A clinic can drift when documentation standards soften without being addressed. A workplace can drift when feedback is avoided because morale is fragile. A training program can drift when students are reassured without being prepared. A leadership team can drift when difficult conversations are delayed until the pattern becomes culture.

Accountability in systems is not about finding someone to blame. It is about refusing to let unclear standards become normal.

It asks: What pattern are we reinforcing? What expectation has not been clarified? What responsibility has been avoided? What support is missing? What follow-through is needed? What harm may occur if we keep calling this compassion?

Those questions protect people.

Unclear standards do not stay neutral. They become culture.

They protect clients from vague care. They protect staff from resentment and confusion. They protect developing professionals from being underprepared. They protect leaders from mistaking likability for integrity.

Systems without accountability may feel easier in the moment. They become more expensive over time.

Avoided truth collects interest.

Punishment focuses on suffering.

Accountability focuses on ownership, repair, learning, and future practice.

Punishment asks, "How do we make this hurt enough?" Accountability asks, "What happened, what belongs to whom, what needs repair, and what needs to change?" That keeps accountability from becoming cruelty and compassion from becoming avoidance.

It names what happened.

It identifies responsibility.

It distinguishes intent from impact.

It invites repair.

It clarifies what needs to change.

It preserves the person's dignity while refusing to erase the behavior.

This is the balance.

The person is not reduced to the mistake. The mistake is also not ignored to protect the person.

In personal growth, accountability asks:

"What belongs to me here?"

That question is simple.

It is also uncomfortable.

Many people avoid it by moving to extremes.

One extreme is blame avoidance.

Nothing is mine.

It was my anxiety.

It was my trauma.

It was my stress.

It was my childhood.

It was the other person's tone.

It was the situation.

It was the timing.

It was how I was triggered.

These factors may matter.

They may explain the reaction.

They may provide necessary context.

They do not automatically remove responsibility.

The other extreme is shame collapse.

Everything is mine.

I ruin everything.

I am terrible.

I cannot do anything right.

I am the problem.

Everyone would be better off without me. This may sound like accountability, but it often avoids the actual work by turning responsibility into identity collapse. Now the focus shifts from repair to reassurance. The person who needs to take ownership becomes the person everyone must comfort.

That is not accountability. That is shame taking over the room. Accountability as compassion chooses a steadier path.

It says:

"My feelings make sense, and my behavior still matters."

"My history matters, and my choices still have impact."

"My pain is real, and I am still responsible for repair." "I can understand why I reacted that way, and I can still practice differently next time."

This is emotional strength. It allows people to face themselves without self-destruction. In relationships, accountability is what makes repair possible.

Without it, conflict becomes circular.

One person names hurt.

The other explains intent.

The first person repeats impact.

The second person becomes defensive.

The conversation turns into a debate over whether the hurt should count.

Nothing gets repaired.

Accountability interrupts that loop.

It says:

"I did not intend to hurt you, and I can see that I did." "I was overwhelmed, and I still should not have spoken to you that way."

"I avoided the conversation, and that made things worse." "I can explain what was happening for me without using it to erase what happened for you."

That kind of ownership builds trust.

Not because the person never makes mistakes.

The person can face them. In clinical work, accountability is equally essential. This is a professional integrity issue, not just a relational preference. Accountability in clinical care protects the client from treatment that feels supportive while leaving harmful patterns untouched. Accountability in supervision protects developing clinicians from being reassured into underdevelopment. Accountability in workplace systems protects standards, documentation, scope, and follow-through. Accountability to clients and communities protects the trust placed in the field. When accountability disappears, care may still sound compassionate, but the work loses its shape. Clients deserve compassion for the patterns that developed in response to pain, fear, trauma, family systems, symptoms, and survival.

Accountability protects trust

Trust does not only depend on warmth. It depends on whether people can believe that truth will be handled honestly. In therapy, clients need to trust that care will not become collusion. In supervision, developing clinicians need to trust that feedback will be given early enough to help them grow. In leadership, teams need to trust that standards mean something. In relationships, people need to trust that impact can be named without the whole connection collapsing.

Accountability protects that trust because it keeps truth in the room.

When accountability disappears, people often compensate by guessing. They guess what is allowed. They guess what matters. They guess whether a pattern will be addressed. They guess whether repair is possible. Over time, guessing weakens trust because clarity is absent.

Compassionate accountability says, "We can tell the truth here." It says, "This matters enough to name." It says, "You are not reduced to this behavior, and this behavior still needs attention."

That is why accountability belongs inside compassion, not outside it.

They also deserve treatment that helps them build responsibility. A client who avoids every difficult task needs validation and behavioral movement. A client who harms relationships during emotional intensity needs understanding and accountability. A client who repeatedly misses appointments needs curiosity and expectations. A client who uses diagnosis as exemption needs respect and clarity. A client who resists exposure needs empathy and a plan. Accountability does not mean the clinician becomes cold. It means the clinician refuses to collude with avoidance. That is part of protecting the work.

Supervision requires the same standard.

Developing clinicians need support.

They need room to learn.

They need space to ask questions, make mistakes, reflect, and build confidence.

They also need accountability.

Documentation matters.

Ethics matter.

Scope matters.

Punctuality matters.

Follow-through matters.

Clinical judgment matters.

Feedback matters.

A supervisee who is never held accountable may feel supported, but they are not being prepared. Support without standards does not build competence.

It builds dependency or drift.

Leadership requires the same thing.

A leader who avoids accountability to stay liked may preserve short-term comfort while weakening the system. A leader who uses accountability without compassion may create fear. A leader with compassion and a spine creates clarity. They can say, "I care about you, and this expectation still matters."

"I understand this is difficult, and we still need follow-through."

"I want to support your growth, and I need to address the pattern."

This is not harsh.

It is honest.

Accountability is also necessary in the private relationship a person has with themselves. Self-accountability is not self-attack. It is the ability to tell yourself the truth without abandoning yourself.

"I am avoiding."

"I am overexplaining."

"I am blaming."

"I am not following through."

"I am asking for confidence while refusing repetition."

"I am calling this peace, but it might be fear."

"I am waiting to be ready because trying would make the outcome real."

These are uncomfortable sentences.

They are also doorways.

You cannot change what you will not name. You cannot repair what you will not own. You cannot build confidence while treating every honest self-observation as shame.

Accountability as compassion says:

"Tell the truth. Stay kind. Take responsibility. Practice differently." That is the sequence. Not shame. Not blame. Not excuses. Not collapse. Truth. Kindness. Responsibility. Practice. This is how confidence grows. Not because you become someone who never gets it wrong. You become someone who can respond when you do.

That is sturdier than perfection.

Much more human.

Practice Point

Notice This

Where do you avoid accountability by explaining, blaming, collapsing into shame, or focusing only on intent? Look for places where repair or change keeps getting delayed.

Try This

Name one responsibility that belongs to you without attacking yourself. Use this structure: "I can understand why I did this, and I am responsible for that."

Measure This

Did your accountability lead to repair, clarity, follow-through, or changed behavior? Accountability becomes compassion when it creates movement without shame.

Chapter 15: Functioning as the Metric of Progress

A plant is not healthier because you learned the names of its roots.

I am unfortunately the kind of person who wants to understand every root before touching the watering can. This chapter is my loving confrontation of that tendency.

The roots matter; they are just not the whole garden.

Knowing the root system matters. Understanding what happened underground matters. Naming the soil, the drought, the damage, the missing nutrients, and the conditions that shaped growth can be important. Sometimes it is necessary. Sometimes nothing above the surface can make sense until someone understands what has been happening below it.

Eventually, health has to show up somewhere.

Not perfectly. Not immediately. Not in a dramatic time-lapse where everything blooms on command. Over time, something has to become more alive, more workable, more rooted, more able to receive light.

Healing is similar.

Insight matters. Language matters. Validation matters. Understanding why something has been hard can be deeply compassionate. If the roots are endlessly studied and the life above the soil keeps withering, the work is not finished.

Healing should change how life is lived.

Not all at once.

Not perfectly.

Not in a straight line.

Over time, healing should affect functioning. This is where modern conversations about mental health sometimes lose their shape.

A person may gain insight.

They may learn language.

They may feel validated.

They may understand their childhood, their attachment patterns, their anxiety, their trauma responses, their relational wounds, their nervous-system activation, their avoidance, and the many reasons they became who they are.

That can be meaningful.

It can be necessary.

It can be powerful.

Insight is not the same as progress. Validation is not the same as change. Awareness is not the same as capacity.

Progress has to show up somewhere.

In behavior.

In choices.

In relationships.

In responsibilities.

In distress tolerance.

In repair.

In boundaries.

In follow-through.

In functioning.

Functioning as the metric of progress does not mean feelings do not matter. Worth and functioning have to be separated. Clinical diagnosis itself attends not only to symptoms, but also to distress, impairment, duration, and context (American Psychiatric Association, 2022).

Functioning needs context

Functioning should never be interpreted without context. A person living with significant illness, poverty, grief, trauma, disability, unsafe housing, active crisis, or limited support may have a very different functional baseline than someone with more stability and resources. Compassion requires that context be taken seriously.

Context should refine the question, not erase it.

The question is not, "Why are you not functioning like someone else?" The better question is, "What would meaningful movement look like for you, in this context, with this support, at this point in time?"

For one person, that may mean returning to work. For another, it may mean showering twice a week. For another, it may mean reducing avoidance by answering one message. For another, it may mean asking for supervision before the issue escalates. For another, it may mean eating one meal, making one appointment, or staying in one hard conversation.

Functioning as a metric does not flatten people into productivity. It asks whether the work is helping life become more livable.

That is a very different standard.

Worth is inherent.

Worth cannot be earned by functioning

This line has to be protected carefully. A person is not more worthy because they are productive, employed, organized, emotionally regulated, clinically stable, physically active, relationally available, or easy to support. Worth is not earned by output. It is not lost during symptoms. It does not disappear in crisis. It does not shrink when functioning does.

Worth is inherent; functioning can be discussed without turning it into a moral verdict.

That is the freedom of separating the two. We can say, “You are worthy,” and also ask, “Is your life becoming more workable?” We can say, “You deserve compassion,” and also ask, “What support would help you re-enter the parts of life that matter?" We can say, "This season has been hard," and also ask, "What is one realistic sign of movement?"

When worth and functioning are fused, any question about behavior feels like an attack on identity. When they are separated, functioning becomes information we can use with care.

Functioning is data. A person's value does not rise and fall with productivity, symptom severity, employment status, energy level, or how much they can accomplish in a day. At the same time, functioning tells us something important about whether life is becoming more workable. Separating worth from functioning allows us to be compassionate without becoming vague. Feelings matter deeply. A person's internal experience should not be dismissed simply because they are still getting things done. High functioning does not always mean healthy. Some people are performing survival very well. Some people can produce, achieve, caretake, lead, and appear composed while internally unraveling.

Sometimes it just means the spreadsheet is color-coded while the person using it is internally held together with tape and caffeine.

Ask me how I know.

Functioning cannot be the only measure. It must be one of them. If a person feels increasingly validated but their life becomes increasingly small, something is incomplete. If a person has more language but less capacity, something is incomplete. If therapy helps someone understand avoidance but avoidance continues to run the schedule, something is incomplete. If a student knows the theory but cannot apply feedback, something is incomplete. If a professional can explain burnout but cannot set a boundary or adjust behavior, something is incomplete. If a relationship has endless processing but no repair, something is incomplete.

Functioning asks the question that comfort often avoids:

"What are you becoming able to do?"

That question is rude only because it is useful.

That question can feel confronting.

It is also clarifying.

Can you open the email?

Can you attend the appointment?

Can you tolerate the conversation?

Can you set the boundary?

Can you follow through?

Can you ask for help without collapsing?

Can you receive feedback?

Can you repair?

Can you practice exposure?

Can you meet responsibilities?

Can you return after a setback?

Can you act in alignment with values while discomfort is present? These questions are not meant to shame. They are meant to locate the work. The goal is not to pretend symptoms do not exist. The goal is to see whether the person is building capacity in the presence of them.

This matters because feeling can fluctuate.

Functioning gives another data point.

A person may feel anxious and still attend the meeting. That is progress. A person may feel guilty and still hold the boundary. That is progress. A person may feel depressed and still complete one small necessary task. That is progress. A person may feel ashamed and still repair the relationship.

That is progress. A person may feel uncertain and still ask the question. That is progress. A person may feel activated and still remain respectful.

That is progress.

The feeling did not disappear.

The person's relationship to the feeling changed.

That is what functioning reveals. In therapy, this is essential. A client may report feeling better in session, but the clinician also has to ask what is changing outside the room.

Are panic symptoms still dictating behavior?

Is avoidance decreasing?

Are relationships becoming more honest?

Is sleep improving?

Is the client engaging responsibilities?

Are boundaries being practiced?

Is exposure happening?

Is distress tolerance increasing?

Is the client becoming more capable?

This does not mean progress is always visible immediately.

Some seasons are slow.

Some treatment work begins with stabilization.

Some clients are dealing with severe impairment, unsafe environments, active crisis, grief, trauma, poverty, illness, or systems that make functioning harder.

Functioning must be assessed with context. Context should not erase the question.

It should refine it. Progress for one person may be returning to work. For anxiety, progress may mean avoidance decreases. For depression, progress may mean behavioral activation increases in small, realistic ways. For trauma, progress may begin with stabilization before moving toward broader functioning. For relationships, progress may mean repair happens sooner and resentment has less room to grow. For supervision, progress may mean documentation improves, feedback is integrated, and follow-through becomes more reliable. Different contexts require different measures. The point is not to force one definition of functioning onto everyone. The point is to ask whether the work is moving somewhere.

Insight has to transfer

One of the clearest signs that growth is happening is transfer. The insight begins leaving the page, the session, the journal, the conversation, or the training room and starts showing up in life.

A person does not only understand that they avoid conflict. They practice one honest sentence.

They do not only understand that guilt follows boundaries. They hold one boundary while guilt is present.

They do not only understand that feedback activates shame. They receive one piece of feedback and return to the work.

They do not only understand that depression steals motivation. They take one small behavioral step before motivation arrives.

Transfer is where confidence begins to trust the work.

Without transfer, insight can become another place to hide. A person may explain beautifully and live unchanged. That is not a failure of insight. It is a sign that insight has not yet become practice.

Functioning asks whether transfer is happening.

Progress for another may be leaving the house twice a week. Progress for another may be reducing compulsions. Progress for another may be eating one meal. Progress for another may be completing documentation on time. Progress for another may be staying in one hard conversation without shutting down. Progress for another may be asking for supervision before a clinical issue escalates. Progress is not the same size for everyone.

Progress still needs a direction. Functioning as the metric of progress keeps healing connected to life. It prevents therapy from becoming endless explanation.

It prevents confidence from becoming aesthetics.

It prevents support from becoming stagnation.

It prevents systems from confusing comfort with outcomes. It prevents the person from mistaking insight for transformation. This is also where professional integrity matters. In mental-health care, we have to be willing to ask whether our interventions are helping. Not whether they sound compassionate. Not whether they feel aligned with current language trends.

Not whether they avoid discomfort.

Are they helping?

Is the client becoming more capable?

Is functioning improving where improvement is realistic?

Is avoidance decreasing?

Is distress tolerance growing?

Is the work moving?

If not, we have to be honest.

That honesty protects the client.

It protects the clinician.

It protects the field.

It protects the work from becoming vague.

Functioning also matters in everyday confidence.

Many people want to feel better about themselves.

That desire is human. Confidence grows most reliably when people begin doing things that make self-trust possible.

Follow through.

Keep one promise to yourself.

Complete one task.

Have one honest conversation.

Set one boundary.

Practice one skill.

Return one message.

Take one step toward the thing you keep circling. Self-esteem without functioning can become fragile because it depends on mood. Self-trust grows through action. When your behavior begins to match your values, confidence has somewhere to root. Not because you feel amazing all the time. You know you can count on yourself more often.

That is sturdy.

This is why functioning is not shallow.

It is not about productivity worship.

It is not about ignoring emotional life.

It is not about measuring worth by output.

A person's worth is not determined by functioning.

Progress often is.

Worth is inherent.

Functioning is clinical, relational, behavioral, and practical data.

Both truths can coexist. I have had seasons where the most honest question was not, "Do I understand myself?" but "Is my life becoming more workable?" That question can be humbling. It is also clarifying; and while it may be terrifying, it does not decide my worth. It tells me where care, structure, support, or practice may be needed next. You are worthy when you are struggling. You are also responsible for noticing whether your life is becoming more workable. You are worthy when you are symptomatic. You are also allowed to build capacity. You are worthy when you need support. You are also capable of practicing one next step.

That question has ruined more than one polished explanation for me. I can make something sound very reasonable when I want to. The harder, better question is whether the explanation is helping me live with more honesty, capacity, and follow-through.

Compassion protects worth.

The spine measures movement.

Together, they keep growth honest.

Practice Point

Notice This

Where do you have insight without movement? Look for areas where you can explain the pattern clearly, but your functioning has not changed.

Try This

Choose one area of functioning to strengthen. Make it concrete: one task, one behavior, one conversation, one follow-through, one exposure step.

Measure This

Track what changed in behavior, not only in feeling. Did your life become slightly more workable? Did your capacity expand? Functioning gives confidence evidence.

Chapter 16: Emotional Adulthood as the Goal

Feelings deserve a seat at the table.

They just do not get to flip the table and call it authenticity.

They bring information. They tell us when something hurts, matters, threatens, disappoints, overwhelms, or needs attention. They can reveal wounds we have ignored, needs we have minimized, boundaries we have avoided, grief we have not named, and desires we have tried to outgrow.

Feelings deserve to be heard.

They do not get to chair the entire meeting.

When emotion becomes the only authority in the room, everything else gets pushed aside: responsibility, values, repair, discernment, timing, impact, and the actual human beings affected by what we do next. Emotional adulthood does not mean kicking feelings out of the room. It means letting them speak without handing them the gavel, the agenda, and full control over the vote.

Emotional adulthood is not the absence of emotion. It is the ability to remain responsible while emotion is present. That matters because emotional adulthood is often misunderstood.

Being unbothered is not the same as being mature. Sometimes it is just avoidance with better posture.

Some people hear it as coldness.

Detachment.

Suppression.

Never needing help.

Never crying.

Never being affected.

Never feeling insecure, anxious, angry, ashamed, jealous, lonely, disappointed, or wildly tempted to send a paragraph that should have remained between you, God, and the notes app.

That is not emotional adulthood.

That is emotional performance.

Emotional adulthood is not pretending you do not feel.

It is not never needing help.

It is not being unbothered.

It is not perfection.

It is not having the best tone in every conversation.

It is not never getting activated.

It is not becoming so contained that no one knows what you need. Emotional adulthood is responsibility in the presence of feeling. I have no interest in becoming a person who feels nothing. That has never been the goal. I want to remain tender, moved, convicted, amused, affected, and fully human. I just do not want every feeling becoming the person in charge of the meeting.

I have absolutely given feelings the microphone before. I have let fear present a full agenda, let shame take minutes, and let urgency try to adjourn before wisdom arrived. Emotional adulthood is learning that every part of me can speak, but not every part of me gets to lead.

It is not becoming so composed that nothing touches you. It is not spiritual bypassing, clinical jargon, productivity, politeness, or having the best response in every conflict. Emotional adulthood is the practiced ability to feel deeply without making your feelings the sole authority over your behavior.

It means emotion gets a voice. It does not get the only vote. This is the final pillar because it integrates the others. Capability gives you the belief that discomfort can be tolerated.

Some feelings will argue with the minutes. Let them. They still do not get to rewrite the whole policy.

This is where my internal committee files several objections.

Boundaries give you structure.

Accountability gives you responsibility.

Functioning gives you a measure of movement. Emotional adulthood brings those pieces into daily life.

It looks like emotion with responsibility:

Emotional adulthood is not emotional perfection

The point is not to stop reacting. The point is to build a more responsible relationship with reaction.

You may still get defensive. Emotional adulthood notices and returns.

You may still feel jealous. Emotional adulthood tells the truth without becoming controlling.

You may still feel angry. Emotional adulthood chooses not to punish someone with that anger.

You may still feel ashamed. Emotional adulthood resists the urge to collapse into self-hatred and instead asks what needs repair.

You may still feel anxious. Emotional adulthood does not let anxiety write every decision.

The difference is not that emotions disappear. The difference is that emotion is no longer treated as permission to abandon responsibility.

That is a hard standard, but it is not a cold one. It allows humanity. It expects ownership. It knows people can be deeply affected and still accountable for what they do next.

Shame without collapse.

Guilt without boundary abandonment.

Anxiety without avoidance.

Sadness without hopelessness.

Hurt without retaliation.

Need without entitlement.

Support without surrendering responsibility.

"I am anxious, and I can still act."

"I am angry, and I can still choose not to harm."

"I am ashamed, and I can still repair."

"I am sad, and I can still care for myself."

"I am disappointed, and I can still communicate clearly."

"I am overwhelmed, and I can still ask for help responsibly."

"I am triggered, and I am still responsible for what I do next."

That last sentence is hard.

It is also necessary.

Being emotionally activated explains something.

It does not excuse everything.

A person can be genuinely hurt and still respond poorly. A person can be overwhelmed and still cause harm. A person can have a reason and still need to repair. A person can be struggling and still need to communicate. A person can have symptoms and still need to practice responsibility. This is not a lack of compassion.

It is what makes relationships possible. Without emotional adulthood, relationships become organized around emotional intensity. The loudest feeling gets the most authority. The most dysregulated person sets the terms. Conflict becomes unsafe because no one knows how to remain responsible inside discomfort. Repair becomes rare because shame takes over. Boundaries collapse because guilt becomes too persuasive. Feedback becomes impossible because defensiveness enters the room before curiosity can sit down. Over time, people become careful instead of honest. They manage reactions instead of addressing patterns. They avoid truth because emotional fallout is too costly.

That is not intimacy.

That is emotional hostage-taking with better lighting.

Emotional adulthood creates another option. It allows people to have feelings without making everyone else responsible for preventing them.

It allows conflict without destruction.

It allows repair without collapse.

It allows boundaries without punishment.

It allows accountability without shame.

It allows closeness without emotional fusion.

It allows people to remain separate and connected at the same time.

This is difficult work.

It is also freeing.

A person practicing emotional adulthood does not need everyone to agree with them in order to feel real. They do not need every boundary to feel good. They do not need every conversation to end in reassurance. They do not need every feeling to be resolved immediately. They do not need discomfort to disappear before they can behave according to their values.

They can pause.

They can reflect.

They can own.

They can repair.

They can stay.

They can leave when needed without turning every exit into a performance. They can say, "I need support," without making someone else responsible for their entire internal world. This is confidence at its most mature.

Not the confidence of being admired. The confidence of being responsible for yourself. Emotional adulthood is built in small moments.

Not during the easy parts. Anyone can seem emotionally mature when nothing is being asked of them. The real practice begins when something activates you.

The private practice no one sees

A lot of emotional adulthood happens before anyone else knows there was a choice point. It happens in the ten seconds before you answer the text. It happens when you delete the defensive paragraph and write the honest sentence instead. It happens when you notice the urge to shut down and ask for a pause rather than disappearing. It happens when you want reassurance but choose to sit with uncertainty for a little longer. It happens when you admit, “I am hurt,” without turning hurt into a weapon.

Those moments are small, but they are not minor.

They are where your emotional habits are being trained.

Every time you pause, name the feeling, and choose responsibility, you are practicing adulthood. Every time you let intensity make the decision, you are practicing something else.

No one gets this perfectly. Perfection is not the goal. Returning is the goal.

When someone says no.

When feedback stings.

When plans change.

When you feel misunderstood.

When someone does not respond quickly.

When a boundary disappoints you.

When you are wrong.

When you are embarrassed.

When old fear enters a new room. When you have to choose between immediate relief and long-term integrity.

Those moments reveal the work.

Not because they define you permanently.

They show what you have practiced. If you have practiced avoidance, you may escape. If you have practiced defensiveness, you may explain. If you have practiced shame, you may collapse. If you have practiced control, you may tighten. If you have practiced emotional adulthood, even imperfectly, you may pause.

That pause is powerful.

It creates room for choice.

Choice is where adulthood lives.

Not in never reacting.

In returning to responsibility after you do.

This matters personally.

It matters clinically.

It matters professionally.

It matters culturally.

A culture without emotional adulthood will confuse discomfort with harm, disagreement with danger, accountability with cruelty, boundaries with rejection, and feelings with facts. A field without emotional adulthood will soften standards to avoid rupture, overvalidate to avoid complaint, and treat activation as a reason to stop rather than a signal to guide carefully. A relationship without emotional adulthood will become fragile under the weight of ordinary tension. A person without emotional adulthood will keep asking the world to become smaller so they do not have to build capacity. That is why this pillar is the goal.

Not because adults should be emotionless.

Growth requires responsibility.

Emotional adulthood is the ability to bring your full humanity into the room without making your humanity an excuse to abandon integrity.

It says:

"My pain matters."

"My choices matter."

"My needs matter."

"My impact matters."

"My boundaries matter."

"My responsibility matters."

All at once.

Not one truth canceling the others.

All of them held together.

That is compassion with a spine.

Soft enough to tell the truth about pain. Strong enough to tell the truth about responsibility.

Gentle enough to honor history.

Clear enough not to be ruled by it.

Warm enough to stay human.

Structured enough to keep growing.

This is what confidence ultimately requires.

Not the absence of fear.

Not constant self-esteem.

Not the perfect nervous system.

Not a life without hard conversations.

Not a personality polished into permanent calm. Confidence requires the practiced belief that you can meet life with honesty, responsibility, support, and capacity.

That is emotional adulthood.

That is the work.

It is built one response at a time.

Practice Point

Notice This

Where do emotions take over responsibility? Look for moments where anxiety, anger, shame, guilt, fear, or sadness becomes the reason behavior is excused instead of understood.

Try This

In one activated moment, practice a pause before responding. Name the feeling, name the responsibility, and choose one action that aligns with your values.

Measure This

Did you remain responsible while feeling? Emotional adulthood grows when emotion is allowed to exist without becoming the only authority in the room.

Compassion with a Spine is not a softer name for toughness.

It is not a prettier name for discipline.

It is not a clinical slogan or a personal-growth aesthetic.

It is a framework for building people, relationships, systems, and work that can hold both care and truth.

Capability over fragility.

Boundaries as care.

Accountability as compassion.

Functioning as the metric of progress.

Emotional adulthood as the goal.

Together, these pillars protect growth from becoming vague.

They protect compassion from becoming passive.

They protect accountability from becoming cruel.

They protect confidence from becoming performance.

They protect healing from becoming avoidance.

Part IV moves from framework to lived practice.
A framework only matters if it changes how we
show up.

A framework that never touches Tuesday afternoon is just an expensive thought.

PART IV

Practicing Capacity in Real Life

A framework only matters if it changes how we live.

Not just how we think.

Not just how we talk.

Not just how accurately we can name patterns, identify wounds, explain symptoms, or describe what should be different.

Those things matter.

They are not the whole work.

The work is what happens next.

After the insight.

After the validation.

After the diagnosis.

After the boundary language.

After the realization that avoidance has been running more of the room than you wanted to admit. After the moment you understand, with uncomfortable clarity, that confidence will not grow inside a life organized around escape. Part IV is about practice. This is where the philosophy has to become behavior. Not because behavior is the only thing that matters, but because behavior is where the framework becomes lived.

Not performance; practice. That is true even in the making of this book. The work did not become real because I thought about it dramatically enough. It became real because I kept returning to the page, one imperfect section at a time, while my brain offered a rotating menu of doubt, urgency, excitement, and "maybe reorganize the whole thing again for sport."

The repeated, ordinary, often unglamorous decisions that build capacity in real life.

In work.

In relationships.

In conflict.

In exposure.

In responsibility.

In the private moments where you decide whether to shrink or engage. Practicing capacity does not mean becoming endlessly productive, emotionally bulletproof, socially fearless, perfectly regulated, or spiritually above needing a snack and a minute. It means learning to meet real life with more steadiness. It means building the ability to do what matters while discomfort is present. It means using compassion as support, not as permission to disappear from the work. Confidence does not become real because we admire the concept. It becomes real because we practice the behaviors that give it evidence. This section moves the framework into daily life.

Growth does not stay theoretical for long.

Eventually, it asks for a decision.

Chapter 17: Work, Competence, and Expectations

Work is supposed to feel challenging. That is not a flaw in the system. It is part of how competence is built. This does not mean work should consume a person, exploit them, ignore reasonable limits, tolerate toxic leadership, or demand endless self-sacrifice while calling it professionalism.

That is not competence.

That is dysfunction with a badge.

The badge does not make dysfunction developmental. It just makes it easier to scan at the door.

I do mean a badge. Possibly laminated.

There are unhealthy workplaces.

There are unreasonable expectations.

There are leaders who confuse pressure with development. There are systems that ask people to carry too much with too little support. Those realities should not be minimized. Not all discomfort at work is evidence of harm. This is where exploitation and expectation have to be separated. Exploitation ignores limits, context, support, workload, safety, and humanity. Expectation develops capacity through clear standards, appropriate challenge, feedback, and support.

Development needs structure

Work is not supposed to be free of discomfort. It is supposed to be structured enough that discomfort can become development. That structure matters.

A challenging role can build competence when expectations are clear, feedback is available, support is appropriate, and the person has room to learn. The same role can become damaging when expectations are vague, workload is unreasonable, leadership is inconsistent, and every request is treated as a test of loyalty.

"Hard" is not enough information.

Hard with structure can develop skill.

Hard without support can become exploitation.

Hard with feedback can build competence.

Hard with humiliation can create fear.

Hard with clear standards can strengthen confidence.

Hard with moving targets can exhaust it.

Professional growth requires challenge, but challenge must be held inside a structure that makes learning possible.

Exploitation consumes.

Expectation strengthens.

A healthy workplace or training environment should not be free of discomfort. It should be structured enough that discomfort can become development. Some discomfort is the cost of learning. Some pressure is the weight of responsibility.

Some uncertainty means you are new. Some feedback means you are being developed. Some stress means you are being asked to stretch. Some challenge is not a sign that you are misaligned. It is a sign that you are growing. In many modern conversations about work, discomfort is treated as a warning that something is wrong. Stress is interpreted as proof of poor fit. Feedback is experienced as personal rejection. Expectations are reframed as unfairness. Pressure is treated as inherently harmful.

Sometimes those interpretations are accurate.

Sometimes they are not.

Competence cannot develop without challenge. You cannot become skilled only doing what already feels easy. You cannot become confident professionally while avoiding every arena where confidence would need to be built. You cannot become a steady leader, clinician, teacher, creator, employee, partner, or professional without repeated contact with uncertainty, feedback, mistakes, correction, and responsibility.

Competence requires exposure.

Not reckless exposure.

Not abandonment.

Not "sink or swim" leadership with a motivational poster stapled to the wall.

Real exposure.

Supported practice.

Clear expectations.

Honest feedback.

Repetition.

Repair.

Learning.

The discomfort of being new.

The discomfort of being corrected.

The discomfort of not knowing everything yet. The discomfort of being seen while you are still developing. Many people confuse that discomfort with incapability.

They feel anxious and think, “I am not ready.”

They feel uncertain and think, “I should not be here.”

They receive feedback and think, “I am failing.”

They make a mistake and think, “This means I cannot do this.”

They feel pressure and think, “This must be unhealthy.” Maybe. Or maybe they are at the edge of growth. This is where confidence and competence become linked.

Confidence follows competence.

Competence follows repetition.

Repetition requires discomfort.

The order matters.

If you wait to feel confident before building competence, you may stay stuck in the doorway. Professional confidence is not built by avoiding difficulty. It is built by surviving difficulty with structure, humility, support, and practice. I did not become confident in this field because I skipped the uncomfortable parts. I became more confident because supervisors, professors, colleagues, clients, mistakes, hard cases, documentation, feedback, and responsibility kept requiring me to grow. Some of that felt affirming. Some of it felt deeply inconvenient to my ego. All of it built something that reassurance alone could not. This applies across roles. The same pattern shows up in performance conversations, clinical documentation, supervision, leadership, imposter feelings, and the question of whether to stay or leave. Sometimes people stay too long in harmful systems because they think endurance proves strength. Sometimes people leave too soon because the discomfort of development feels like proof they do not belong.

Feedback is part of competence

Feedback often feels personal because work is not just task performance. Work can touch identity, pride, fear, ambition, shame, and the desire to be seen as capable. That is especially true in helping professions, leadership, teaching, clinical work, and creative work where the person and the product can feel intertwined.

Feedback is one of the places competence develops.

A clinician needs feedback to sharpen judgment. A supervisor needs feedback to improve leadership. An employee needs feedback to understand expectations. A creator needs feedback to learn what is landing and what is not. A student needs feedback because learning without correction is usually guessing with confidence.

The goal is not to enjoy feedback. The goal is to stop treating discomfort during feedback as proof that feedback is harmful.

Good feedback should be specific, behaviorally anchored, and connected to growth. Poor feedback may be vague, shaming, punitive, or inconsistent. Again, discernment matters.

If all feedback becomes threat, competence has nowhere to refine itself.

Both require discernment.

The question is not simply, "Is this hard?"

The question is, "Is this hard in a way that develops capacity, or hard in a way that damages it?" A new clinician does not become confident by reading every textbook until uncertainty disappears. They become confident by learning, practicing, consulting, receiving supervision, making thoughtful decisions, tolerating feedback, and gradually developing clinical judgment. A leader does not become confident by avoiding hard conversations. They become confident by having them, repairing when needed, refining their approach, and learning how to hold both people and standards. An employee does not become confident by avoiding every task that activates insecurity. They become confident by engaging tasks long enough to develop skill.

A creator does not become confident by waiting until the work is immune to criticism. They become confident by making, sharing, adjusting, and continuing. Work exposes the places where confidence is still conditional.

Conditional confidence says:

"I can feel okay if I already know what I am doing."

"I can participate if I am sure I will succeed."

"I can speak if I know everyone will agree."

"I can accept feedback if it does not make me feel bad."

"I can grow if growth does not require embarrassment."

That is not sturdy confidence.

That is comfort with better lighting.

Sturdy confidence says:

"I can be new and still learn."

"I can receive feedback and remain intact."

"I can make a mistake and repair."

"I can ask questions without making uncertainty mean incompetence."

"I can be challenged without collapsing into shame."

"I can grow into the role."

Work often becomes one of the clearest places where fragility patterns appear.

Avoiding feedback.

Declining opportunities because they feel activating.

Reducing effort before trying.

Calling all pressure harm.

Interpreting correction as cruelty.

Leaving roles before competence has time to develop.

Needing constant reassurance to continue.

Mistaking discomfort for misalignment.

Again, sometimes leaving is wise.

Sometimes the environment is unhealthy.

Sometimes the expectations are unreasonable.

Sometimes the role is not a fit. Sometimes the body is giving accurate information. Compassion with a Spine does not tell people to endure dysfunction and call it growth.

It asks for discernment. Is this harmful, or is this hard? Is this exploitation, or is this expectation? Is this feedback cruel, or is this feedback uncomfortable? Is this role misaligned, or am I afraid to be new? Is this burnout, or is this the result of unclear boundaries and avoidance of necessary change? Is this too much, or have I not built the skill yet? Those questions matter because the wrong answer can cost you. If you call harm "growth," you may stay somewhere damaging. If you call growth "harm," you may keep leaving before capacity develops. Both errors matter. Professional integrity requires the ability to distinguish between the two.

So does personal confidence.

The goal is not to normalize overwork.

The goal is to normalize development: feedback, repetition, correction, responsibility, and the discomfort of being evaluated while you are still learning. It includes discovering that you can be imperfect and still competent.

"Am I becoming more capable?"

"Am I following through more consistently?"

"Am I receiving feedback more effectively?"

"Am I asking for support earlier?"

"Am I tolerating the discomfort of learning?"

"Am I growing into responsibility?"

"Am I avoiding the parts of work that would build skill?" Those questions bring confidence back to evidence. A person can feel anxious and still be building competence. A person can feel uncertain and still be learning well. A person can feel exposed and still be developing. A person can feel challenged and still be in the right room. The feeling is not the only data point.

The pattern matters.

Are you expanding?

Are you practicing?

Are you becoming more capable?

Are you engaging the work honestly?

That is where confidence grows.

Not because work becomes easy.

You become sturdier inside the challenge.

Practice Point

Notice This

Where are you avoiding professional growth because it feels uncomfortable? Look for avoided feedback, delayed tasks, declined opportunities, or places where you leave mentally before you have practiced long enough to build skill.

Try This

Choose one work-related stretch point and engage it directly. Ask for feedback, start the task, request supervision, clarify the expectation, or stay with the learning curve instead of retreating from it.

Measure This

Track competence, not comfort. Did you practice? Did you follow through? Did you learn? Did your capacity expand even slightly?

Chapter 18: Relationships That Can Tolerate Tension

Healthy relationships are not relationships without tension. They are relationships that can survive it. Peace and the absence of discomfort are not the same thing.

No disagreement.

No disappointment.

No hard conversations.

No misunderstandings.

No boundaries that create friction.

No feedback that lands awkwardly.

No emotional activation.

No moment where someone has to say, “That hurt,” “That did not work for me,” “I need something different,” or “We need to talk.” That version of peace may feel appealing.

It is also not intimacy.

It is a very tidy loneliness.

It is often avoidance.

Peace includes honesty.

The cost of false peace

False peace is expensive because it requires people to keep paying with honesty. One person does not say what hurt. Another person pretends the pattern is fine. Someone else keeps lowering a need so the relationship does not have to stretch. Everyone may be calm, but the calm is being purchased with silence.

That is not peace. It is emotional debt.

Emotional debt has aggressive interest rates.

Sooner or later, the debt collects. It may collect as resentment, distance, sarcasm, withdrawal, overexplaining, irritability, or the quiet grief of realizing you are known only in the parts of yourself that do not inconvenience anyone.

Real peace is different. Real peace can tolerate truth. It may not feel peaceful at first because honesty often disrupts the old arrangement. If the relationship has capacity, honesty can create a deeper peace than avoidance ever could.

Tension is not automatically the enemy of connection. Sometimes it is the doorway to a more honest one.

Avoidance avoids truth. Peace may be quiet, but it is not built on everyone swallowing what needs to be said. Avoidance can look peaceful because no one is naming the tension. The difference is what the silence is protecting. Relationships require tension because relationships involve difference.

Different needs.

Different histories.

Different limits.

Different expectations.

Different emotional rhythms.

Different wounds.

Different ways of interpreting silence, tone, timing, conflict, closeness, distance, and the apparently catastrophic meaning of a text message that only says "okay." Tension is not automatically a sign that the relationship is unsafe. Sometimes tension is the relationship becoming more honest. I have had to learn that honest tension is not always relational failure. Sometimes it is the moment a relationship stops performing peace and starts telling the truth. That does not make the conversation easy. I remain very much in favor of hard conversations coming with snacks and a reasonable processing window. Avoiding all tension does not protect connection. It often protects distance. This is difficult for people who learned to associate tension with danger. If conflict in your history meant yelling, withdrawal, punishment, chaos, abandonment, humiliation, or emotional volatility, then ordinary disagreement may not feel ordinary. It may feel threatening. Your body may react before your current mind has time to assess the actual situation.

This matters.

It deserves compassion.

It also needs practice.

If every relational tension is treated as proof of danger, relationships will become organized around avoidance.

People will say less.

Ask for less.

Risk less.

Clarify less.

Repair less.

They may keep the peace, but they lose honesty. When honesty disappears, resentment usually moves in quietly and starts unpacking. A relationship that cannot tolerate tension becomes fragile.

Everyone becomes careful.

Careful with needs.

Careful with limits.

Careful with honesty.

Careful with feedback.

Careful with disappointment.

Careful with emotional truth.

Careful not to activate the other person.

Careful not to require too much.

Careful not to be inconvenient.

Carefulness can look loving for a while.

Eventually, it becomes lonely. Real connection requires enough capacity for truth. That does not mean every feeling needs to become a conversation. It does not mean every irritation deserves a meeting. It does not mean honesty should be used as an excuse to be unkind.

Some thoughts can remain thoughts.

Some reactions are yours to regulate.

Some conversations need timing, maturity, and more than a caffeine-based will to confront everyone before noon.

Important patterns need words.

Needs need words.

Limits need words.

Repair needs words.

Accountability needs words.

Trust needs words and follow-through.

Relationships that can tolerate tension allow people to be real without becoming reckless.

They make room for sentences like:

"I care about you, and I need to be honest."

"That hurt me."

"I understand your intention, and the impact was still difficult."

"I need a boundary here."

"I was wrong."

"I got defensive."

“I need support, but I do not need you to fix this for me.” “I need space, and I will come back to the conversation.”

“I love you, and this pattern cannot continue.”

Those sentences require capacity.

They also build it.

Each honest conversation gives the relationship information.

Can we survive difference?

Can we repair?

Can we hear each other without collapsing?

Can we tolerate disappointment? Can we stay connected when comfort is not immediate? Can we be honest without becoming cruel? Can we be hurt without becoming destructive?

This is where confidence grows relationally.

Not from never having conflict.

From learning that conflict does not have to end connection.

Not from never disappointing anyone.

From learning that disappointment can be tolerated.

Not from always being understood.

From learning that misunderstanding can be clarified.

Not from being perfectly regulated. From learning that activation can be repaired. This is emotional adulthood in relationship form. It allows two people to remain human at the same time.

That may sound obvious.

It is not always practiced.

In many relationships, only one person is allowed to struggle at a time. One person's feelings take up all the oxygen. One person's activation becomes the center. One person's discomfort determines what can be discussed. One person's avoidance sets the pace of the relationship.

That is not mutuality.

That is emotional imbalance.

Compassion with a Spine asks relationships to hold more than one truth.

Your pain matters.

Their impact matters.

Your boundary matters.

Their boundary matters.

Your history matters.

Their limits matter.

Your needs matter.

Their capacity matters.

Your feelings matter.

Your responsibility matters.

All at once.

This is harder than choosing one truth and weaponizing it.

It is also healthier.

A relationship without accountability becomes enabling.

A relationship without compassion becomes harsh.

A relationship without boundaries becomes blurry.

A relationship without repair becomes brittle.

A relationship without tension is often not honest enough yet. This applies to romantic relationships, friendships, families, teams, supervision relationships, and clinical work. Therapy itself is a relationship that must tolerate tension. A clinician may need to challenge avoidance.

A client may feel misunderstood.

A repair conversation may be necessary.

A boundary may need to be clarified.

Feedback may need to be given. If the therapeutic relationship cannot tolerate tension, the work will become limited to what feels comfortable.

That is not enough.

The same is true in supervision.

Supervisees need support, but they also need feedback. Supervisors need to be compassionate, but they also need to hold standards. If tension is avoided, growth is delayed. In families, tension often reveals old roles.

The fixer.

The peacekeeper.

The scapegoat.

The responsible one.

The emotional one.

The invisible one.

The one who is expected to absorb everything because they always have.

Boundaries interrupt those roles.

Honesty interrupts those roles.

Growth interrupts those roles.

That interruption will create tension.

The presence of tension does not mean the growth is wrong. It may mean the pattern is being challenged. Confidence cannot be built only privately. At some point, confidence has to enter relationships.

It has to speak.

It has to clarify.

It has to repair.

It has to say no.

It has to say yes honestly.

It has to let others have feelings without becoming responsible for managing every one of them. It has to stay kind without disappearing.

That is not easy.

It is practice.

A relationship that can tolerate tension is not one where everyone always gets it right. It is one where people are willing to return.

Return to honesty.

Return to repair.

Return to responsibility.

Return to the conversation with more humility.

Return without pretending nothing happened. Return without making the rupture the whole story. This is where rupture and repair matter.

Rupture is not automatically failure; unrepaired rupture is where the damage grows. Repair teaches the relationship that disconnection does not have to be permanent. It teaches people that harm can be named.

Impact can be owned.

Trust can be rebuilt through behavior.

Patterns can change.

Repair is not a speech.

Repair after the apology

After an apology, the real repair often begins. That is the part people sometimes miss. They apologize and expect the discomfort to end, but repair is not only the sentence that acknowledges harm. Repair is the pattern that follows.

If the behavior continues, the apology becomes less meaningful each time. If the person apologizes but resents the impact, repair stays shallow. If they demand immediate trust, the apology becomes another form of pressure. If they make the other person manage their shame, the repair turns back into self-protection.

Real repair asks for patience. It allows the other person to need time. It understands that trust is rebuilt through consistency, not urgency. It does not control the timeline because discomfort is inconvenient.

This matters because many relationships are not destroyed by one rupture. They are worn down by unrepaired repetition. The same issue returns. The same apology is made. The same behavior follows.

Eventually, the apology stops sounding like repair and starts sounding like part of the pattern.

A relationship that can tolerate tension also has to tolerate the time repair requires. That is part of emotional adulthood. It is part of trust. It is part of learning that connection is protected by changed behavior, not by rushing everyone back to comfort.

It is not an apology designed to end discomfort quickly.

It is not "I am sorry you feel that way."

It is not "I already apologized, so why are you still upset?" It is not "Can we just move on?" when moving on means skipping responsibility. Repair requires ownership. In romantic relationships, repair may mean naming the impact instead of arguing over intention. In families, repair may mean respecting a boundary without punishing the person for setting it. In friendships, repair may mean returning to the conversation instead of letting distance become the solution. In supervision, repair may mean addressing feedback directly and adjusting practice. In therapy, repair may mean naming an alliance rupture rather than pretending the session simply moved on.

Repair is a confidence practice

Repair builds relational confidence because it teaches people that rupture does not have to mean ending, disappearing, punishing, or pretending. It teaches the nervous system that conflict can move somewhere other than destruction.

That kind of learning matters for people who grew up around volatility, silence, withdrawal, or relationships where apologies were performances rather than change. Repair may feel unfamiliar. It may feel humiliating. It may feel like giving up power. It may feel like danger.

Healthy repair is not surrender; it is responsibility.

It says, "Connection matters enough for me to tell the truth about my part." It says, "Trust matters enough for me to change behavior, not just explain intention." It says, "This relationship matters enough for us to tolerate discomfort instead of making avoidance the rule."

That is why relationships that can repair become sturdier. Not because they never break, but because they know how to return.

Repair is not about making tension disappear quickly. It is about making trust possible again through honesty and changed behavior.

Specificity.

Changed behavior.

Tolerance for the other person's timeline.

Willingness to understand impact.

The humility to not control how quickly trust returns.

This is uncomfortable. It is also where relational confidence grows. When you know you can repair, conflict becomes less terrifying. When you know you can hold boundaries, honesty becomes less dangerous. When you know you can tolerate disappointment, people's reactions become less controlling. When you know you can stay connected to yourself, relationships become less likely to require self-abandonment. That is confidence through compassion with a spine.

Not a relationship without discomfort.

A relationship with enough capacity to move through it.

Practice Point

Notice This

Where do you confuse tension with danger? Look for relationships where you stay silent, over-explain, avoid conflict, soften boundaries, or manage someone else's emotions to preserve peace.

Try This

Choose one honest but kind sentence you have been avoiding. Say it with clarity, not aggression. Focus on truth, responsibility, and the next step.

Measure This

Did the relationship have more clarity after the conversation? Did you stay connected to yourself while allowing tension to exist?

Chapter 19: Growth and Exposure

Growth is not something you arrive at.

It is something you practice. In clinical settings, exposure is a structured intervention. It is used to treat anxiety, obsessive-compulsive patterns, trauma-related avoidance, panic, and other fear-based patterns when appropriate. It is planned, paced, supported, and repeated (Barlow, 2002; Craske et al., 2014). Outside of clinical settings, the same principle still matters.

Not as a protocol.

As a way of understanding growth.

Exposure is the decision to engage with what is safe but uncomfortable, repeatedly, until your capacity expands. Clinically, exposure is more than "facing your fear." It is a planned, repeated approach to safe but feared or avoided experiences, with attention to learning, avoidance reduction, and the person's ability to remain engaged long enough for new information to form. For the everyday reader, the principle is simpler: exposure teaches the body through experience that discomfort can be survived without escape. That teaching cannot happen if the person never approaches the feared situation.

Small enough to do, large enough to matter

The most useful exposure step is often smaller than pride wants and larger than avoidance prefers.

Which is annoying, because both pride and avoidance have very strong opinions.

Pride wants a cinematic leap. Avoidance wants a weighted blanket and no follow-up questions.

If the step is too small, it may not touch the fear enough to create learning. If the step is too large, it may overwhelm the person and strengthen the belief that approach is unsafe. The practice is finding a step that creates contact without chaos.

Small enough to do.

Building an exposure ladder without making it a mountain

One reason people avoid growth is that they turn the first step into the whole mountain. They think if they are afraid of being seen, the first step must be public visibility. If they are afraid of conflict, the first step must be the hardest conversation. If they are afraid of the gym, the first step must be a complete routine in front of everyone. If they are afraid of writing, the first step must be a polished chapter.

That is often too much.

An exposure ladder gives fear something more honest to practice. It breaks approach into steps. Not so the person can avoid forever at the bottom, but so the nervous system can learn gradually enough to stay engaged.

For creative visibility, the ladder might begin with writing privately, then sharing with one trusted person, then posting a small piece, then tolerating feedback, then sharing more consistently. For boundaries, it might begin with noticing resentment, then writing the sentence, then saying it in a lower-stakes relationship, then holding it when guilt rises. For body confidence, it might begin with a walk, then a home workout, then entering the gym briefly, then completing one simple routine.

The ladder is not a loophole. It is a structure for practice.

The goal is movement, not perfection. Repetition, not drama. Learning, not proving.

Large enough to matter.

That sentence can guide a lot of growth.

If the gym feels impossible, the first step may be walking through the door, not completing an entire workout. If the conversation feels impossible, the first step may be writing the honest sentence and reading it aloud to yourself. If sharing creative work feels impossible, the first step may be sending it to one safe person. If grief feels impossible, the first step may be sitting with one memory for five minutes without numbing.

The step is not symbolic. It is instructional. It teaches the body that approach is possible.

It is not forcing yourself into harm.

It is not flooding yourself for the sake of proving strength.

It is not ignoring your limits.

It is not abandoning wisdom.

It is not treating trauma like a motivational obstacle course.

Exposure without care can be reckless.

Care without exposure can become avoidance.

Compassion with a Spine holds both.

It asks:

What is safe enough to approach?

What support is needed?

What step is small enough to practice?

What pattern is avoidance reinforcing?

What would help capacity grow?

Avoidance narrows the world.

Exposure expands it.

Avoidance says, “I cannot handle this.”

Exposure says, “I can practice handling this in a supported way.”

Avoidance says, “Relief now.”

Exposure says, “Capacity over time.”

Avoidance says, “Stop because this is uncomfortable.”

Exposure asks, “Is this unsafe, or is this the edge where growth begins?” This applies everywhere. It applies to social anxiety when being seen feels intolerable. It applies to fitness and body confidence when the gym feels like a room full of witnesses. It applies to conflict when one honest sentence feels dangerous. It applies to creative visibility when sharing the work feels exposing. It applies to a career stretch when the next role asks you to be new again. It applies to grief when feeling the loss seems like it might swallow you. It may even apply to faith, worship, or community re-entry after a season where returning feels vulnerable. The context changes.

Exposure also teaches what avoidance was costing

Approach does not only reduce fear. It can reveal what avoidance has been protecting you from and what it has been keeping you from.

Avoiding the gym may protect you from feeling exposed, but it may also keep you from strength, energy, confidence, and the experience of inhabiting your body with more trust. Avoiding conflict may protect you from tension, but it may also keep you from honesty, repair, and deeper connection. Avoiding creative visibility may protect you from criticism, but it also keeps your work from becoming real in the world. Avoiding grief may protect you from pain, but it may also keep you from love that deserves to be mourned honestly.

Exposure is not only about fear going down.

It is about life opening back up.

That is why it belongs in a book about confidence. Confidence grows when your world has more doors than exits.

The principle remains: approach what is safe enough to practice.

The conversation you keep avoiding.

The application you keep delaying.

The boundary you keep softening.

The feedback you keep dodging.

The task you keep postponing.

The room you keep not entering.

The grief you keep outrunning.

The dream you keep calling unrealistic because wanting it would require risk. Each avoided thing teaches your nervous system something.

It teaches, "We escape this."

Each approached thing teaches something, too.

It teaches, "We can meet this."

That does not mean the first attempt feels good.

It may feel awful.

It may feel awkward.

It may feel clumsy, sweaty, emotionally inconvenient, and not at all like the inspirational version of growth people put in captions.

That is fine.

Exposure is not measured by elegance.

It is measured by engagement.

Did you approach?

Did you stay?

Did you practice?

Did you return?

Did you allow the discomfort to rise and fall without letting avoidance decide everything?

That is the work. In anxiety treatment, exposure helps the brain learn that feared situations can be survived without escape, avoidance, reassurance, or compulsive control (Barlow, 2002; Craske et al., 2014). The point is not to make anxiety vanish immediately. The point is to build new learning through repeated experience. The same principle shows up in everyday confidence. If you fear being seen, practice being seen in small ways. If you fear feedback, practice asking for it and staying present. If you fear conflict, practice one honest sentence. If you fear failure, practice doing something where imperfection is guaranteed. If you fear rejection, practice asking without controlling the outcome.

If you fear responsibility, practice follow-through. If you fear disappointment, practice letting someone be disappointed without abandoning your values. Growth does not require a grand leap. Often, the leap becomes another reason to avoid. People make the step so large that the nervous system rejects it before practice begins.

"I need to change my whole life."

"I need to become completely confident."

"I need to overhaul every habit."

"I need to fix my entire relationship pattern."

"I need to heal everything before I begin."

No.

Begin smaller.

Small enough to do.

Large enough to matter.

That is the exposure edge.

I have used this in embarrassingly ordinary ways: taking the walk, opening the document, posting the thing, asking the question, starting before I had the perfect plan. None of those moments looked dramatic from the outside. Very few growth moments do. Yet each one created a small piece of evidence that I was not as incapable as fear was trying to suggest.

A step that is not so tiny it avoids the fear entirely, but not so large that it overwhelms the system. For one person, that may be opening the bill.

For another, sending the application.

For another, walking into the gym.

For another, asking for clarification in a meeting. For another, ending a conversation when yelling starts. For another, letting themselves write badly for fifteen minutes. For another, attending therapy and telling the truth. For another, sitting with grief for five minutes without numbing. For another, receiving help without apologizing for needing it.

The size of the step depends on the person, the pattern, and the context, but the principle remains the same.

Practice approach.

Not perfectly.

Repeatedly.

This is where many people misunderstand growth. They think the first step should make them feel more confident.

Sometimes it does.

Often, it does not.

Sometimes the first step simply teaches you that you did not die, the ceiling did not collapse, and the group chat did not convene a tribunal about your worth. That is still evidence. The nervous system is not always dramatic in its learning.

Sometimes capacity grows quietly.

The email gets easier.

The conversation gets less terrifying.

The gym feels less foreign.

The boundary becomes less shaky.

The feedback becomes less personal.

The silence becomes less threatening.

The attempt becomes less humiliating.

Repetition changes the relationship.

Not always quickly.

Honestly.

Exposure also reveals where support is needed. If you repeatedly cannot approach something, that information matters.

Maybe the step is too large.

Maybe the fear is connected to trauma.

Maybe the environment is genuinely unsafe. Maybe you need therapy, supervision, medical support, skills training, or practical help. Maybe the approach needs to be paced differently. Compassion with a Spine does not say, "Push harder no matter what." It says, "Let's tell the truth about what is happening and build the right support for the next step." This matters because growth without compassion becomes force.

Compassion without exposure becomes maintenance.

The goal is neither force nor maintenance.

The goal is expansion.

Expansion is not always comfortable.

It is also not chaos. It is intentional contact with what builds capacity. The more you practice approach, the more your world opens. The more you practice avoidance, the more it closes.

That is not a moral judgment.

It is a behavioral reality.

What you practice strengthens.

If you practice escape, escape becomes easier. If you practice engagement, engagement becomes more available. If you practice silence, silence becomes familiar. If you practice honesty, honesty becomes more possible. If you practice waiting to feel ready, waiting becomes the pattern. If you practice beginning while uncertain, movement becomes the pattern. Exposure is the practice of teaching your life that discomfort is not the end of the story. It is the practice of allowing confidence to grow from evidence. It is the practice of becoming someone who can move toward what matters without needing fear to leave first.

This does not make fear irrelevant.

It makes fear less in charge.

That is growth.

Not the absence of fear, but a different relationship with it.

Practice Point

Notice This

What safe but uncomfortable thing have you been avoiding repeatedly? Look for places where avoidance has reduced immediate distress but narrowed your life over time.

Try This

Choose one exposure step. Make it small enough to do and meaningful enough to matter. Practice approach once, then repeat it.

Measure This

Did you move toward the thing instead of away from it? Did your behavioral range expand? Exposure builds confidence through repeated approach.

Chapter 20: Practicing Confidence Before You Feel Ready

Readiness is overrated.

I say this with love and also with the full awareness that I personally would like seven confirmation signs before doing anything brave.

Not always.

There are times when preparation matters.

Training matters.

Safety matters.

Planning matters.

Competence matters.

Support matters.

Wisdom matters.

Please do not interpret this chapter as permission to make dramatic life decisions at 11:47 p.m. because you had one emotional breakthrough, two sips of water, and a playlist that made you feel powerful.

Readiness has its place.

Preparation and readiness are not the same thing.

Readiness can move the goalpost with the confidence of someone who never planned to play.

Readiness can be a moving finish line

When readiness is run by fear, it keeps changing the requirements. First, you need more information. Then more confidence. Then more time. Then a better plan. Then better timing. Then proof that it will work. Then reassurance that no one will misunderstand you, reject you, criticize you, or notice that you are new.

By then, readiness is no longer wisdom. It is a moving finish line.

Preparation has an endpoint. Avoidant readiness does not.

Preparation says, "I have what I need for the next step." Avoidant readiness says, "I need to remove all uncertainty before I begin."

That is impossible.

Every meaningful step contains some uncertainty. Applying, creating, apologizing, dating, returning, launching, speaking, healing, leading, and changing all require a little movement before the body feels fully convinced.

Confidence is built by crossing that threshold with support, not by waiting outside it forever.

Preparation builds capacity. Readiness can become avoidance when it delays action indefinitely. Preparation asks, “What do I need in order to take the next step wisely?” Avoidant readiness asks, “How do I keep waiting until risk disappears?”

One creates movement. The other creates a more convincing pause. Readiness can also become a very polished form of avoidance.

“I am not ready yet.”

“I need more time.”

“I need to feel more confident first.”

“I need to heal more.”

“I need to know exactly how this will go.”

“I need to wait until life calms down.”

“I need to understand the whole plan.”

“I need to become the kind of person who can do that.”

Sometimes those sentences are true. Sometimes they are fear with a clipboard. The problem with waiting to feel ready is that many forms of readiness only develop through practice.

You become ready by beginning. I wish I could tell you I waited until I felt completely ready to write this book, but that would be adorable fiction. I began with conviction on social media, then a messy outline, too many thoughts, not enough sleep, and the persistent suspicion that the book was either going to become something real or haunt me forever like an unfinished Google Doc with opinions. Readiness did not arrive first. Repetition did.

The truth is that this book was written by practicing the very thing it teaches: doing the next honest piece before I had full confidence, full certainty, or full emotional permission from the committee in my head.

You become confident by creating evidence. You become capable by engaging the thing that currently feels difficult. You become clearer by taking the next step and learning from it. You become steadier by practicing steadiness in real moments, not imagined ones. This is frustrating because it means growth asks for movement before certainty. It asks you to enter the room while still feeling unsure. It asks you to write the bad draft. It asks you to have the conversation before the perfect words arrive. It asks you to try the class before you feel like someone who belongs there. It asks you to apply before imposter syndrome gives written permission. It asks you to start before your confidence has completed its hair, makeup, legal review, and emotional risk assessment.

You do not need to feel ready to take the next honest step. You need the step to be appropriate.

The next honest step is not always the biggest one. Sometimes practicing confidence looks small on purpose. A small step is not a lesser step when it creates movement. Confidence is often built through small, repeated acts of self-trust. You say you will do something, and you do it. You say you need to pause, and you pause. You say you will try for ten minutes, and you try for ten minutes. You say you will not over-explain, and you stop after the clear sentence. You say you will return to the task, and you return. You say you will ask for help, and you ask. Self-trust grows when your behavior becomes more reliable than your fear.

That reliability is confidence.

Not flashy confidence.

Not the kind that needs an audience. The kind that lets you know you can count on yourself. Tiny promises matter. A person who repeatedly breaks promises to themselves will struggle to feel confident, even if the promises seem small.

Small promises rebuild self-trust

Small promises matter because they are how self-trust is repaired after avoidance. Most people do not lose trust in themselves all at once. They lose it through repeated moments where they say they will begin tomorrow, respond later, set the boundary next time, stop overexplaining soon, or return to the task when life calms down.

The promise may seem small, but the pattern becomes large.

Rebuilding self-trust does not require a dramatic overhaul. In fact, dramatic overhauls often become another avoidance strategy because they are too large to sustain. Self-trust is rebuilt through promises small enough to keep and honest enough to matter.

"I will work on this for ten minutes."

“I will send the message before noon.”

“I will go for the walk even if it is short.”

“I will say no without writing an essay.”

“I will open the document.”

“I will ask for help instead of disappearing.”

Each kept promise tells the body, “My words can become action.” That is confidence at its most basic level. Not glamorous. Not loud. Foundational.

When you miss, repair the promise instead of turning it into proof that you cannot be trusted. Make it smaller. Tell the truth. Return. Self-trust is not built by never missing. It is built by not abandoning yourself when you do.

“I will start tomorrow.”

“I will respond later.”

“I will set the boundary next time.”

“I will go next week.”

“I will stop saying yes when I mean no.”

“I will take care of that soon.”

Each broken promise becomes evidence, too.

The nervous system notices.

Not with cruelty.

With pattern recognition.

When your words to yourself do not become action, self-trust weakens. When your words become action, self-trust strengthens. This does not mean you must become rigid.

Life happens.

Plans change.

Energy shifts.

Responsibilities collide.

Bodies have limits.

Some days are survival days.

Self-trust is not built through perfection.

It is built through honest follow-through and honest repair. If the plan needs to change, tell the truth.

Do not disappear from yourself.

Adjust the plan.

Make it smaller.

Return tomorrow.

Ask for help.

Repair the missed promise.

The issue is not that you sometimes miss. The issue is whether avoidance becomes the pattern and honesty disappears. Practicing confidence before you feel ready also means allowing yourself to be seen in process. This may look like posting content before you feel fully polished. Applying for the job before imposter feelings disappear. Starting therapy before you know how to explain everything. Going to the gym before your body feels acceptable to you. Setting the boundary before guilt is gone. Launching the project before every detail is perfect. Returning to dating, friendship, church, community, or creativity before you feel completely unafraid.

The beginning will feel like beginning

A lot of people are not afraid of doing the thing. They are afraid of being seen at the beginning of the thing.

They are afraid of the first awkward workout, the first uncertain post, the first rough draft, the first honest boundary, the first therapy session where they do not know how to explain themselves, the first attempt after failure, the first conversation after silence, the first version of a dream that is not yet polished enough to defend.

Beginnings are supposed to look like beginnings.

A beginning is not evidence that you are unqualified. It is evidence that you are entering the practice phase. You do not become someone who can by waiting until you already look like someone who can.

You become someone who can by letting the first repetition count.

That first repetition may not impress anyone. It may not even impress you. It still matters because it interrupts the pattern of waiting.

Submitting the work before you can guarantee how it will be received.

These are not reckless leaps. They are practiced entries back into life. This is hard for people who have attached confidence to polish. They do not want to begin until they can look competent. They do not want to speak until the sentence is perfect. They do not want to try until they can guarantee they will be good. They do not want to be witnessed learning. Being seen in process is part of becoming.

No one becomes confident only in private. At some point, growth has to risk visibility.

The first attempt may be awkward.

The first post may not land.

The first conversation may be clumsy.

The first boundary may shake.

The first class may feel uncomfortable.

The first draft may offend every internal editor you have ever developed. That does not mean you are not meant for it.

It means you are beginning. Beginning is allowed to look like beginning. This is especially important for people rebuilding confidence after criticism, failure, rejection, trauma, grief, burnout, body shame, relational wounds, or seasons where life made them feel smaller than they used to be. Rebuilding confidence is not about pretending those experiences did not affect you. It is about creating new evidence after they did.

You may begin more cautiously.

You may need more support.

You may need to pace yourself.

You may need to practice trust in smaller increments.

That is okay.

Small does not mean weak.

Small can be strategic.

A tiny step taken honestly is more useful than a dramatic plan avoided repeatedly. A seed is not unimpressive because it is small; it is only useless if it never gets planted.

Confidence before readiness asks:

"What can I practice now?"

Not someday.

Not when I become a completely different person.

Not when fear disappears.

Now.

What is the next honest repetition?

What is the smallest visible step?

What would create one piece of evidence? What can I do with the capacity I have today?

This does not mean you should ignore growth edges that require more preparation.

Some things need training.

Some conversations need support.

Some clinical work requires supervision.

Some decisions need time.

Some risks are not wise.

Some exposure needs to be paced.

Some wounds need treatment.

Compassion with a Spine is not impulsivity with a cute title.

It is structured courage. Structured courage asks for both honesty and movement. It does not let fear disguise itself as wisdom forever. It also does not let urgency pretend to be bravery. That balance matters. There is a difference between a next step and a dramatic escape.

A next step builds capacity.

A dramatic escape often avoids it.

Quitting everything may feel powerful.

Having one honest conversation may be the actual growth. Buying all the supplies may feel motivating. Doing the first boring repetition may be the actual growth. Planning the perfect routine may feel productive. Keeping one small promise may be the actual growth. Announcing the change may feel exciting. Practicing quietly for two weeks may be the actual growth. Confidence is built where behavior meets repetition.

Not where intention gets applause. Practicing confidence before readiness is not about becoming reckless.

It is about becoming honest.

Honest about fear.

Honest about avoidance.

Honest about capacity.

Honest about what matters.

Honest about the fact that waiting has a cost. Every time you wait to feel ready, ask what waiting is producing.

Is it producing preparation?

Is it producing wisdom?

Is it producing stabilization?

Is it producing support?

Or is it producing more waiting?

That question will tell you a lot. Sometimes waiting is part of the work. Sometimes it is the way we avoid the work. Confidence grows when we learn the difference. You do not need to become fearless. You do not need to become perfectly ready. You do not need to become someone who never doubts, never shakes, never hesitates, never feels exposed, never has to practice.

You need one honest next step.

Then another.

Then another.

That is how readiness is built; not by waiting outside your life, but by entering it with practice.

Practice Point

Notice This

Where are you waiting to feel ready before you act? Look for places where "not yet" has become a long-term pattern.

Try This

Choose one next honest step that does not require full readiness. Make it small, specific, and doable within your current capacity.

Measure This

Did the step create evidence? Did it strengthen self-trust? Confidence grows when you practice before readiness feels complete.

Chapter 21: Protect the Work. Protect the Field. Protect the Person

You Are Becoming.

There is a reason this book began with erosion and ends with practice.

Critique is not enough. Naming the leak matters; eventually someone still has to get the bucket, patch the pipe, and stop staring at the ceiling like it will repair itself.

Eventually someone has to put down the diagnostic flashlight and pick up the tools.

Naming drift matters.

The difference between naming and building

Naming matters because unnamed patterns keep repeating in the dark. Naming is not the finish line. A person can name avoidance and still avoid. A clinician can name drift and still fail to correct it. A leader can name a standard and still refuse to hold it. A relationship can name the rupture and still never repair.

The book cannot end at critique. Naming what has gone sideways only matters if we are willing to build something better.

Critique identifies what is eroding. Construction asks what must be practiced instead. That is the point of protecting the work and the person becoming: not to point at what is wrong forever, but to build enough structure that something better can hold.

The work has to become behavioral. The field has to become clearer. The person has to become more capable. Otherwise, the language becomes a place to gather around the problem without ever changing the pattern.

Protecting the work means naming what is weakening it and then building what strengthens it.

Calling out misinformation matters.

Protecting clinical language matters.

Distinguishing discomfort from harm matters.

Refusing to let avoidance dress itself as healing matters. Critique alone does not build capacity.

It can name what is wrong.

It cannot become the whole work.

The work is construction.

Eventually, someone has to pick up the hammer. Preferably not in a panic, but still.

Building clearer language.

Building stronger clinical standards.

Building steadier relationships.

Building better supervision.

Building more honest workplaces.

Building emotional adulthood.

Building confidence that does not depend on comfort. Building lives that do not shrink around fear. The original call gets larger here. Growing with Confidence names the personal work: confidence is practiced capacity. The Professional Integrity Project names the professional standard: integrity requires protected standards. Compassion with a Spine is the bridge between them. Personal growth and professional integrity are not separate conversations. Both ask what happens when compassion is strong enough to build people instead of simply soothe them.

Protection is not passivity

To protect something does not mean to keep it untouched. Sometimes protection requires movement. Protecting the work may require feedback. Protecting the field may require standards. Protecting clients may require uncomfortable clinical honesty. Protecting the person you are becoming may require you to stop cooperating with the version of comfort that keeps making your life smaller.

Protection is not always soft. It is not always quiet. It is not always agreeable. Sometimes protection sounds like a boundary. Sometimes it sounds like accountability. Sometimes it sounds like a no. Sometimes it sounds like, "This pattern cannot continue." Sometimes it sounds like, "I need help." Sometimes it sounds like, "I am scared, and I am doing the next step anyway."

Protection and practice belong together.

We protect what matters by refusing to let it be weakened by avoidance, drift, silence, or fear. We practice because protection without movement can become preservation of the very thing that needs to change.

Protecting the person you are becoming

Protecting the person you are becoming is not the same as protecting every current comfort. The person you are becoming may need you to stop calling avoidance peace. She may need you to tell the truth about what the old patterns are costing. She may need you to set the boundary, ask the question, send the application, return to the room, or let the work be seen before it feels safe.

She may also need tenderness.

She may need rest, therapy, prayer, friendship, pacing, medical care, supervision, or a slower step. Protecting her does not mean forcing her. It means refusing to abandon her to fear.

Honest ones can.

For clinicians, protecting the work means refusing to let culture redefine care as comfort alone. For everyday readers, protecting the person you are becoming means refusing to let fear become the author of your life. It means noticing where comfort has become costly, where language has become a hiding place, and where the next honest step is asking for your participation. It means remembering that therapy is not simply a place where people feel validated. It is a place where people build capacity.

The bridge becomes the book

This is the bridge that holds the whole manuscript together.

Growing with Confidence names the personal work: confidence is not an aesthetic, a mood, or a performance. It is practiced capacity in ordinary life.

The Professional Integrity Project names the professional standard: care requires precision, accountability, scope, boundaries, and enough integrity to protect the work even when comfort would be easier.

Compassion with a Spine names the philosophy underneath both: people deserve care that honors their pain and still believes in their capacity.

This book is not only about mental health culture, confidence, or clinical drift. It is the foundation underneath all three.

It is a call to stop confusing protection with progress.

It is a call to build people without hardening them.

It is a call to protect the work and the person becoming strong enough to live it.

It means using accurate language.

Holding standards.

Assessing carefully.

Practicing within scope.

Addressing avoidance.

Measuring functioning.

Offering compassion that strengthens instead of colludes. It means tolerating the discomfort of clinical responsibility.

The work deserves that.

Clients deserve that.

The field deserves that.

For students and developing professionals, protecting the field means learning to value precision before performance.

It means asking questions.

Seeking supervision.

Tolerating feedback.

Respecting scope.

Letting uncertainty become a teacher instead of a threat. It means understanding that compassion is not proved by softness alone. It is proved by ethical steadiness. For leaders and supervisors, protecting the work means holding both support and standards. It means not rescuing people out of development. It means not avoiding feedback because discomfort may rise. It means not calling inconsistency compassion. It means building systems where people can grow without the work losing its shape. For individuals outside the field, protecting the person you are becoming means reclaiming growth from a culture that keeps selling you relief while calling it healing.

It means recognizing that confidence is not something you purchase, post, manifest, or wait for. It is something you practice. It means understanding that your pain matters, and your patterns matter, too. Your history matters, and your choices still matter. Your limits matter, and some limits may be able to expand. Your feelings matter, and they do not have to run the room. Your healing matters, and it should help you live more fully, not shrink more beautifully. That is the whole point.

A healed life

is not necessarily an easy life.

It is not a life without anxiety, grief, conflict, responsibility, feedback, discomfort, uncertainty, or moments where you still have to talk yourself through the next right thing. A healed life is a life with more capacity.

More honesty.

More steadiness.

More responsibility.

More room.

More ability to stay connected to yourself while life is being life.

That is confidence.

Not constant certainty.

Not constant calm.

Not constant glow.

Capacity.

The ability to say:

“This is hard, and I can take the next step.”

“This is uncomfortable, and I do not have to disappear.”

“This is painful, and I can seek support without surrendering responsibility.” “This is not what I wanted, and I can still respond with integrity.” “This is scary, and fear does not get the only vote.” That is

Growing with Confidence through Compassion with a Spine.

It is not soft self-help.

It is not clinical coldness.

It is not hustle culture with therapeutic vocabulary.

It is not fragility dressed as healing.

It is the integration of care and structure.

Warmth and truth.

Validation and responsibility.

Support and expectation.

Protection and practice.

Compassion and spine.

This work will not always feel comfortable

Growth rarely does. Comfort was never the goal.

Comfort can be part of healing.

Rest can be part of healing.

Safety can be part of healing.

Softness can be part of healing.

None of them are the whole of healing.

Healing must eventually build capacity.

Confidence must eventually become practiced.

Compassion must eventually become strong enough to tell the truth. The life you are becoming must eventually become larger than the fear that tried to contain it.

So protect the work.

Protect the field.

Protect the people we serve.

Protect the person you are becoming.

Not by avoiding discomfort.

By learning how to move through it with enough compassion to stay human and enough spine to keep growing.

Practice Point

Notice This

What part of you is trying to grow, and what keeps pulling you back into avoidance? Name both honestly.

Try This

Write one sentence that protects the person you are becoming. Make it clear, grounded, and connected to action. For example: "I protect my growth by practicing the hard conversation instead of avoiding it."

Measure This

Did your action protect growth, not just comfort? Did it move you toward capacity, confidence, or integrity?

Practicing capacity in real life means bringing the framework out of theory and into behavior.

Work.

Relationships.

Exposure.

Readiness.

Responsibility.

Confidence grows when compassion becomes strong enough to support action. It grows when we stop asking life to become small enough for fear and begin building enough capacity to meet life with steadiness. This does not happen all at once.

It happens through repetition.

One honest step.

One clear boundary.

One repaired rupture.

One tolerated discomfort.

One followed-through promise.

One moment of choosing growth over avoidance.

That is how confidence becomes lived.

Not performed.

Practiced.

The Life That Grows Back

Growth does not always feel like expansion at first.

Sometimes it feels like discomfort.

Sometimes it feels like grief.

Sometimes it feels like guilt after a boundary.

Anxiety before a step.

Shame after feedback.

Sadness after honesty.

Fear before visibility.

The ache of becoming someone who no longer fits inside the patterns that once kept life predictable. That is part of why people avoid growth.

Not because they are weak.

Growth asks something of us.

It asks us to tolerate the space between who we have been and who we are becoming. It asks us to release the old relief patterns before the new capacity feels fully familiar. It asks us to practice before confidence arrives. It asks us to choose honesty when avoidance would feel easier. It asks us to stop confusing the absence of discomfort with the presence of healing.

That is not easy.

It is also not impossible.

You are not fragile because you have struggled. You are not incapable because you feel deeply. You are not limited to the patterns that helped you survive. You are not required to build an identity around what hurt you. You are not obligated to keep shrinking because shrinking once felt safer than being seen. You are shaped by what you practice.

That truth can be uncomfortable.

It is also hopeful.

If avoidance can be practiced, engagement can be practiced, too. If fear can be reinforced, capacity can be reinforced. If silence can become familiar, honesty can become familiar. If self-abandonment can become a pattern, self-trust can become one, too. If your life has narrowed, it can begin to widen.

Not all at once.

Not without support.

Not without tenderness.

Not without setbacks, old habits, missed attempts, awkward repairs, and moments where you catch yourself halfway into the same pattern and think, "Well. Here we are again." That is allowed. Growth is not proven by never repeating old patterns. Growth is often proven by noticing sooner.

Growth does love a rerun, unfortunately.

Returning faster.

Repairing more honestly.

Avoiding less automatically.

Choosing differently one moment earlier than you used to.

That counts.

A life grows back through repetition.

One honest conversation.

One boundary held.

One task approached.

One apology made without collapse.

One piece of feedback received without self-destruction. One uncomfortable step taken before readiness felt complete. One moment where you let the feeling exist without letting it become the entire decision. One choice to stay connected to yourself when fear wanted you to disappear.

This is not dramatic work.

Most real growth is not.

It is quieter than the reveal.

Less polished than the caption.

More ordinary than the version people like to market. It happens in kitchens, cars, offices, therapy rooms, supervision spaces, classrooms, bedrooms, bathrooms, sidewalks, parking lots, and the exact three feet of floor where you stand trying to convince yourself to do the next right thing. It happens when no one is clapping. It happens when you choose the steady thing. It happens when you stop waiting to feel like the person you are trying to become and begin practicing as her. I am still practicing this. I think I always will be. Not because the work failed, but because becoming is not a one-time achievement. It is a rhythm. A return. A decision made again in the next room, the next conversation, the next uncertain beginning.

That is confidence.

Not performance.

Not constant certainty.

Not never feeling anxious, ashamed, sad, angry, disappointed, exposed, or afraid. Confidence is the lived evidence that you can meet yourself in those moments and still choose with integrity. It is the growing belief that discomfort does not have to decide your life. It is the quiet trust that you can feel deeply and still remain responsible. It is the strength to be soft without collapsing. The courage to be clear without becoming cruel. The humility to be accountable without becoming ashamed. The steadiness to be compassionate without abandoning truth.

That is compassion with a spine. It matters far beyond one person. When one person practices capacity, relationships change.

So begin there. Not perfectly. Not loudly. Not all at once. Begin with the next honest repetition. One decision at a time. One repetition at a time. One brave, ordinary, honest step at a time.

APPENDIX
Putting Compassion with a Spine Into Practice

A framework earns its place when it survives contact with real life. It should still make sense when you are tired, activated, embarrassed, responsible for other people, unsure what the right answer is, or tempted to make the uncomfortable thing disappear as quickly as possible.

Compassion with a Spine was never meant to become another set of phrases that sound good highlighted in a book. The point is practice. Use this appendix as a field guide for the moments where care, honesty, responsibility, and discomfort collide.

Start With the Five-Pillar Check

1. Capability over fragility

Ask: What response helps this person become more capable, not merely less uncomfortable? Support should help someone carry more of their own life over time. If the response consistently removes every demand, consequence, difficult conversation, or opportunity to practice, it may be protecting relief more than growth.

In your own life, ask whether you need protection, practice, or a smaller step. Those are not the same thing. A smaller step can still move forward.

2. Boundaries as care

Ask: What needs to be clear so care does not turn into resentment, confusion, or overfunctioning? A boundary names what you will do, what you can offer, what you cannot offer, or what happens next if a pattern continues.

If the boundary requires another person to think, feel, apologize, agree, or behave exactly as you want before you can be okay, it may be a control attempt wearing boundary language.

3. Accountability as compassion

Ask: What truth needs to stay in the room even if it is uncomfortable? Accountability keeps behavior connected to impact, responsibility, repair, and future choice. It can say: this hurt someone; this did not meet the standard; this pattern cannot continue; this is yours to repair.

Self-compassion does not require pretending your impact does not count because your intentions were good. Mature self-compassion lets you tell the truth without turning the truth into self-destruction.

4. Functioning as the metric of progress

Ask: Is life becoming more workable? Insight matters. Feeling understood matters. Naming patterns matters. Look beyond those things to functioning: relationships, responsibilities, work, routines, decision-making, follow-through, emotional recovery, willingness to engage, and the size of the life a person is able to live.

Progress may still feel messy. Someone can be anxious and functioning better. Someone can be grieving and communicating more honestly. The metric is not constant comfort. The metric is whether capacity is growing.

5. Emotional adulthood as the goal

Ask: What belongs to me here? Emotional adulthood means having feelings without assigning everyone else the job of managing them. It means knowing when to ask for support without turning support into rescue, and letting other adults own their choices and reactions.

The Two Failure Modes

When compassion becomes collusion

Collusion often looks helpful. It may sound validating, protective, generous, patient, flexible, or understanding. The question is what the help reinforces.

Ask: Am I helping someone face reality, or helping them avoid it? Am I supporting a pause with a plan to return, or helping disappearance become the plan? Am I lowering the demand because the demand is genuinely unsafe or unrealistic, or because I do not want to tolerate the person's distress?

Compassion becomes collusion when care starts protecting the pattern that keeps the person stuck.

When spine becomes rigidity

Standards without humanity can become brittle. Accountability without curiosity can become punishment. Boundaries without context can become walls. Capability language can become an excuse to ignore actual limits.

Ask: Am I holding a standard, or proving a point? Have I considered context, capacity, safety, power, history, and what support is actually available? Would I still call this fair if I were not frustrated? A spine gives structure. It is not supposed to become a weapon.

Everyday Life

Most of this work happens in ordinary moments: the unopened email, the appointment that needs to be made, the budget you do not want to look at, the workout that feels inconvenient, the application that feels exposing, or the honest sentence waiting in your throat.

A Compassion with a Spine response often sounds like: I understand why I want to avoid this. I am still going to take the next workable step.

If you are exhausted, ask what rest would actually restore and what can wait without becoming another week of avoidance. If you are anxious, ask what part of the task can be made smaller without making the task disappear. If you are ashamed, ask what repair is available instead of turning shame into an identity.

The point is not to make every day a self-improvement project. The point is to notice the repeated choices that either widen or narrow your life.

Relationships

Relationships expose the framework quickly because another person gets a vote. Boundaries become real when someone dislikes them. Accountability becomes real when repair costs pride. Emotional adulthood becomes real when the other person's reaction is not the one you wanted.

In conflict, ask: What happened? What belongs to me? What belongs to the other person? What needs to happen next? Those questions keep the conversation attached to behavior and repair instead of turning it into a trial about who is the better person.

Compassion may sound like: I understand why you reacted that way. Spine may sound like: the impact still needs to be addressed. Compassion may say: I know this boundary is disappointing. Spine may say: I am not changing it to make the disappointment disappear.

Watch for over-explaining, too. Sometimes explanation creates clarity. Sometimes it is an attempt to secure permission for a boundary you are already allowed to hold.

Work and Leadership

Workplaces are full of situations where compassion and spine get separated. Leaders avoid feedback because they do not want to upset someone. Employees absorb role creep because they do not want to look difficult. Teams build workarounds around one person's inconsistency until the workaround becomes the culture.

For employees, the framework may mean clarifying scope, asking what takes priority, documenting decisions, requesting feedback, or naming when responsibility has been assigned without authority. Professional confidence grows through contact with the work, not through protection from every uncomfortable part of it.

For leaders, it means refusing the false choice between being supportive and holding standards. Clear expectations, timely feedback, role clarity, and consistency are forms of support.

Before rescuing, ask whether the problem is training, clarity, capacity, resources, or accountability. Those require different responses. Doing the work for someone may finish the task; it does not automatically build the person.

Clinical and Supervisory Work

The professional application requires the most precision because the stakes are higher. Compassion with a Spine is not permission to push clients, supervisees, or students past what is clinically, ethically, or developmentally appropriate. Care still has to remain connected to assessment, scope, functioning, skill-building, and responsibility.

For clinicians, ask whether an intervention is reducing suffering in a way that builds capacity or reducing distress in a way that reinforces avoidance. Pacing, stabilization, and accommodation may all be clinically necessary. The question is whether the intervention has a direction.

For supervisors, ask whether support is helping the clinician think more clearly, practice more competently, and take appropriate ownership of the work. Developing professionals need room to ask questions; they also need feedback, standards, documentation, consultation, and correction.

A useful supervision question is: What would protecting the client, the clinician, and the integrity of the work require here? Sometimes the answer is reassurance. Sometimes it is training, consultation, transfer, documentation, remediation, or a direct conversation nobody was hoping to have.

Professional compassion is not proved by how little discomfort exists in the room. It is proved by whether the room can hold truth without losing humanity.

A Quick Decision Check

When you do not have time for a full framework review, ask:

What is the actual problem?

What is unsafe, and what is merely uncomfortable?

What belongs to me?

What support would build capacity rather than replace it?

What boundary or standard needs to be clear?

What repair, responsibility, or next action is still required?

What would functioning look like if this were improving?

What is the next honest step?

The framework is not supposed to give you a perfect answer for every moment. It is supposed to help you choose the next response without abandoning either care or responsibility.

The Framework in One Sentence

Compassion with a Spine means caring about the person enough to tell the truth, hold the structure, protect what matters, and still believe in their capacity to grow.

That includes you.

Keep the soft heart. Keep the strong spine. Then practice.

ACKNOWLEDGMENTS

Writing this book has reminded me, again and again, that no one becomes who they are alone. Every person who grows with confidence does so because someone, somewhere, helped steady them. Someone modeled courage. Someone told the truth. Someone offered grace. Someone held a standard. Someone made room for both softness and strength. This book is rooted in that kind of influence. To my parents; thank you for giving me resilience before I had the language for it. Thank you for the examples of strength, grit, survival, humor, and choosing to grow even when life did not make that easy. Everything I do in this field is rooted in that foundation. Thank you for believing in me, supporting me even when you did not fully agree, and teaching me, in your own ways, what steadiness looks like. Mom, thank you for teaching me emotional regulation long before either of us had the clinical language for it. Dad, thank you for always reminding me that the sun will come up tomorrow. That sentence has carried more weight than you probably know.

To my grandparents: thank you for your quiet steadiness and unconditional support. Your belief in me gave me a sense of capability long before I understood what that meant clinically. To my grandmother; thank you for your wit, sarcasm, courage, and the kind of strength that does not need to announce itself to be felt. To my grandfather; thank you for encouraging my dreams at every stage, whether I was pursuing my master's degree, considering doctoral programs, or exploring paths that stretched far beyond what I could fully see at the time. To my aunts and uncles; thank you for showing up through encouragement, humor, grounding, honesty, and the reminder that family exists across many forms and many seasons of becoming. Thank you for teaching me how to stand up for myself, how to have hard conversations, and how to believe I could do more than I thought.

To my siblings; thank you for being part of the life that shaped me long before this book had a title, a structure, or the audacity to become real. Being the middle of five, with two sisters and two brothers, means I have never lacked witnesses, challengers, history-keepers, or people who knew me before I had language for half of what I now teach. Each of you has been part of the story in ways both obvious and quiet.

To my friends; thank you for being the people who reminded me that there is life outside the work, laughter inside the hard seasons, and steadiness available when I was too deep in my own head to find it quickly. Thank you for listening to ideas, celebrating small milestones, tolerating manuscript updates, telling the truth when I needed it, and helping me stay human while this book became real. Your friendship gave me room to be both driven and tired, excited and overwhelmed, certain and still becoming.

To my professors, both undergraduate and graduate; thank you for challenging me, pushing me, and refusing to let me coast. To those who demanded critical thinking, clinical honesty, ethical precision, and integrity in the work, you shaped the clinician and educator who now writes these pages.

A special thank you to:

Dr. Justin Rueb; University of Wisconsin–Stevens Point

Dr. Cory Clark; The Chicago School of Professional Psychology

Dr. Rodney Harris; The Chicago School of Professional Psychology

You each left a lasting imprint on my development academically, ethically, clinically, and personally. You helped sharpen the part of me that now refuses to separate compassion from standards. To the supervisors and mentors who guided my early training, especially:

Rebecca Ginn, Registered Nurse

Gretchen Ekins, Licensed Clinical Social Worker

Dr. Nicholas Mahoney, Residential Psychiatrist

Casey Coughlin, Licensed Clinical Social Worker

Amy Mitchell, Advanced Practice Social Worker

Eric Costea, Registered Nurse

Amanda Carson, Licensed Social Worker

Thank you for your wisdom, feedback, leadership, steadiness, and the permission to be both human and clinician at the same time. I learned what real supervision is because of you. I learned that the best mentors do not simply reassure; they develop. They do not erase discomfort; they help you build the capacity to work through it. That influence lives in these pages. To my colleagues; especially the ones who sat with me through the hardest cases, the longest days, the emotional weight, and the moments when the work felt heavier than I could hold alone. Thank you for grounding me, laughing with me, challenging me, and reminding me that this field, despite everything, is still worth fighting for. The Professional Integrity Project was born from a fierce love for this work, and that love was shaped by the people who kept showing up inside it.

To the clients, past and present, who trusted me with their stories, their pain, their hope, and their growth; you are the reason this book exists. You taught me courage, honesty, resilience, and the responsibility of holding another person's healing with care and precision. You taught me that confidence is not performance. You taught me that capacity is built in real life, through hard conversations, small steps, setbacks, repair, and the brave decision to keep practicing. You changed me. I carry that with reverence.

To Charles; my partner, my steady place, my compass. Thank you for your honesty, grounding, patience, humor, and belief in me when I doubted myself most. Thank you for listening to endless drafts, endless processing, endless ideas, and the many versions of "wait, I think I figured it out" that came before this book found its shape. Your support is woven into this work in ways both visible and invisible.

To the mentors in this field who modeled what I now call compassion with a spine; thank you for showing me that directness and kindness are not opposites. Thank you for proving that clinical care can be warm without becoming vague, firm without becoming harsh, and deeply human without losing its standards.

To The Professional Integrity Project community; thank you for meeting the call to protect the work, protect the field, and protect the people we serve. Thank you for every comment, conversation, message, reflection, and moment where this language helped name something you had been feeling but had not yet found words for. The PIP began as language, but it became a movement because other people recognized the standard underneath it.

To the Growing with Confidence community; thank you for giving me a place to practice the softer side of this work out loud. You have reminded me again and again that confidence is not built through performance, perfection, or pretending we have it all together. It is built in ordinary moments: choosing the next honest step, returning to yourself, learning to be seen, rebuilding after hard seasons, and finding small ways to grow from grounded to glowing. Thank you for receiving the reminders, reflections, imperfect attempts, beauty conversations, wellness rhythms, faith-rooted encouragement, and real-life confidence work with such openness. This community helped me see that compassion with a spine does not only belong in clinical rooms or professional conversations. It belongs in daily life, in self-trust, in body confidence, in routines, in relationships, in faith, and in the quiet places where women are learning to stop shrinking and start becoming.

To God; thank you for the calling, the conviction, the clarity, and the courage to write what needed to be written, even when it was uncomfortable. Thank you for every door that opened, every door that closed, every season that built capacity, and every reminder that this work is not mine alone. This book is my offering back.

Lastly, every clinician working to protect the integrity of this field, every student learning how to hold compassion and standards together, every person rebuilding confidence after seasons of shrinking, and every reader trying to reclaim healing from misinformation, fear, avoidance, or shame; this book is for you.

Thank you for doing the work. Thank you for practicing.

Thank you for growing with confidence through compassion with a spine.

CONTINUE THE WORK

This book was never meant to end as a pile of highlighted sentences. The point is practice.

Growing With Confidence

The community side of this work: confidence in ordinary life, self-trust, body confidence, routines, relationships, faith, and learning to stop shrinking.

Instagram: @growing.with_confidence

The Professional Integrity Project™

The professional side: clinicians, supervisors, students, leaders, and organizations protecting the work without confusing comfort with care. Consultation, mentorship, training, and professional resources live here.

Instagram: @professionalintegrityproject

Resources + Apparel

Frameworks, books, journals, trainings, practical tools, and Compassion With a Spine apparel:

TheProfessionalIntegrityProject.com

Soft heart. Strong spine.

Protect the work. Protect the field. Protect the people we serve.™

References

American Psychiatric Association. (2022). Diagnostic and statistical manual of mental disorders (5th ed., text rev.). American Psychiatric Association Publishing. https://doi.org/10.1176/appi.books.9780890425787

Bandura, A. (1977). Self-efficacy: Toward a unifying theory of behavioral change. Psychological Review, 84(2), 191–215. https://doi.org/10.1037/0033-295X.84.2.191

Barlow, D. H. (2002). Anxiety and its disorders: The nature and treatment of anxiety and panic (2nd ed.). Guilford Press.

Craske, M. G., Treanor, M., Conway, C. C., Zbozinek, T., & Vervliet, B. (2014). Maximizing exposure therapy: An inhibitory learning approach. Behaviour Research and Therapy, 58, 10–23. https://doi.org/10.1016/j.brat.2014.04.006

Gross, J. J. (1998). The emerging field of emotion regulation: An integrative review. Review of General Psychology, 2(3), 271–299. https://doi.org/10.1037/1089-2680.2.3.271

Hayes, S. C., Strosahl, K. D., & Wilson, K. G. (2012). Acceptance and commitment therapy: The process and practice of mindful change (2nd ed.). Guilford Press.

Linehan, M. M. (2015). DBT skills training manual (2nd ed.). Guilford Press.

Masten, A. S. (2001). Ordinary magic: Resilience processes in development. American Psychologist, 56(3), 227–238. https://doi.org/10.1037/0003-066X.56.3.227

Skinner, B. F. (1953). Science and human behavior. Macmillan.

Tangney, J. P., & Dearing, R. L. (2002). Shame and guilt. Guilford Press.